ALASKA'S BEARS

ALASKA GEOGRAPHIC.

VOLUME 20, NUMBER 4 / 1993

The Alaska Geographic Society

To teach many to better know and more wisely use our natural resources

EDITOR
Penny Rennick

PRODUCTION DIRECTOR
Kathy Doogan

STAFF WRITER
L.J. Campbell

BOOKKEEPER/DATABASE MANAGER
Vickie Staples

CUSTOMER SERVICE REPRESENTATIVE
Patty Bliss

POSTMASTER: Send address changes to
ALASKA GEOGRAPHIC®
P.O. Box 93370
Anchorage, Alaska 99509-3370

ISBN: 1-56661-014-1 (paper);
1-56661-015-X (hardback)

PRICE TO NON-MEMBERS THIS ISSUE: $18.95

PRINTED IN U.S.A.

COVER: *Otto, a 5-year-old male, finds a comfortable perch near Mikfik Creek, in McNeil River State Game Sanctuary. He ran to safety on this rock when a larger male chased him off the flats by the river. He was about 30 feet from the photographer and other visitors on the observation pad. Otto spent several hours here, napping, rolling around to scratch his back, and watching people watching bears. (Alissa Crandall)*

PREVIOUS PAGE: *These polar bear cubs huddle on the ice of the Beaufort Sea while researchers put a radio collar on their mother. Female polar bears in Alaska often have two cubs in a litter every third year. (S.C. Amstrup)*

FACING PAGE: *This black bear enjoys a dandelion salad. (Harry M. Walker)*

ALASKA GEOGRAPHIC® (ISSN 0361-1353) is published quarterly by The Alaska Geographic Society, 639 West International Airport Road, Unit 38, Anchorage, AK 99518. Second-class postage paid at Anchorage, Alaska, and additional mailing offices. Copyright © 1993 by The Alaska Geographic Society. All rights reserved. Registered trademark: Alaska Geographic, ISSN 0361-1353; Key title Alaska Geographic.

THE ALASKA GEOGRAPHIC SOCIETY is a non-profit organization exploring new frontiers of knowledge across the lands of the Polar Rim, putting the geography book back in the classroom, exploring new methods of teaching and learning—sharing in the excitement of discovery in man's wonderful new world north of 51°16'.

SOCIETY MEMBERS receive *ALASKA GEOGRAPHIC*®, a quality magazine that devotes each quarterly issue to monographic in-depth coverage of a northern geographic region or resource-oriented subject.

MEMBERSHIP in The Alaska Geographic Society costs $39 per year, $49 to non-U.S. addresses. ($31.20 of the $39 is for a one-year subscription to *ALASKA GEOGRAPHIC*®.) Order from The Alaska Geographic Society, P.O. Box 93370, Anchorage, AK 99509-3370; telephone (907) 562-0164, fax (907) 562-0479.

SUBMITTING PHOTOGRAPHS: Please write for a list of upcoming topics or other specific photo needs and a copy of our editorial guidelines. We cannot be responsible for unsolicited submissions. Submissions not accompanied by sufficient postage for return by certified mail will be returned by regular mail.

CHANGE OF ADDRESS: The post office does not automatically forward *ALASKA GEOGRAPHIC*® when you move. To ensure continuous service, please notify us six weeks before moving. Send your new address, and, if possible, your membership number or a mailing label from a recent *ALASKA GEOGRAPHIC*® to: The Alaska Geographic Society, P.O. Box 93370, Anchorage, AK 99509-3370.

MAILING LISTS: We occasionally make our members' names and addresses available to carefully screened companies and publications whose products and activities may be of interest to you. If you prefer not to receive such mailings, please advise us, and include your mailing label (or your name and address if label is not available).

COLOR SEPARATIONS BY: Graphic Chromatics

PRINTED BY: Hart Press

ABOUT THIS ISSUE: Bears and Alaska just seem to go together, and with all the new information being gathered by bear researchers, we decided an issue devoted exclusively to Alaska's bears might intrigue Alaska Geographic Society members. To put together the text, we turned to some of the state's foremost wildlife researchers. Bruce H. Baker of Juneau wrote the black bears chapter and reviewed the brown and polar bear sections. Bill Sherwonit of Anchorage contributed the brown bear and bears and humans chapters and the smaller sections on prime bear-viewing areas in the state. Staff writer L.J. Campbell tackled the polar bear chapter under the close scrutiny of researchers Steven Amstrup and Gerald Garner of the U.S. Fish and Wildlife Service. Juneau writer Pat Costello wrote the chapter on LaVern Beier, one of Southeast's premier wildlife technicians, and Roger Kaye of Fairbanks prepared the section on tracking the grizzlies of northern Alaska.

Many shared information with us about their experiences with Alaska's bears, and for their cooperation and assistance we thank Dr. John Schoen, senior conservation biologist with the Alaska Department of Fish and Game; Larry Aumiller, manager of McNeil River State Game Sanctuary; Vic Barnes, wildlife researcher with Kodiak National Wildlife Refuge; Paul Schaefer with the U.S. Forest Service's Pack Creek bear-viewing area; Jack Lentfer, now retired and formerly in charge of Alaska's polar bear research for U.S. Fish and Wildlife Service; and John Hechtel of the Alaska Department of Fish and Game in Fairbanks who conducts much of the state's bear research in northern Alaska.

CONTENTS

5

Black Bears

17

Brown/Grizzly Bears

39

Polar Bears

57

Bear-Viewing
57 Anan Creek
59 Pack Creek
62 O'Malley River
64 Brooks River
67 McNeil River

71

Bears and Humans

81

LaVern Beier, Brown Bear Man

87

On the Trail of the Brown Bear

94

ALASKA GEOGRAPHIC® Newsletter

110

Index

111

Bibliography

BLACK BEARS

BY BRUCE H. BAKER

Editor's note: *A former longtime employee of the Alaska Department of Fish and Game and the U.S. Forest Service, Bruce is now a forest resource consultant and freelance writer.*

Alaska's Native people knew bears to be highly intelligent and to have excellent hearing. If they refrained from saying the animals' names aloud it was out of respect for them. The black bear was, nevertheless, known as *s'eek* to Southeast Alaska's Tlingit Indians, as *shoh zhraii* to the Athabaskan Gwich'in of the upper Yukon and Porcupine rivers, and as *iyyagrig* to the Inupiat Eskimo.

The American black bear (*Ursus americanus*) is the smallest of North America's bears. Like the others, it is a member of Ursidae, a family that started out as a branch of the dog family, Canidae, about 25 million years ago. The earliest bears were forest dwellers, like today's

A bluish "glacier" bear in Glacier Bay National Park and Preserve exhibits a rare color phase of the black bear. (John Hyde)

black bear, but they were smaller. Although the ancestors of the American black bear are thought to have crossed the Bering Land Bridge about 500,000 years ago, the species is now found only in North America.

DESCRIPTION

The black bear is compact and stoutly built with fairly massive legs and feet, a moderate-size head with a brown, tapered nose and long nostrils. The lips can be moved with considerable dexterity. The small ears are rounded and erect. The small eyes are brown in adults and blue in cubs. The fairly straight facial profile helps distinguish it from the grizzly or brown bear (*Ursus arctos*). The tail is about three inches long. Adult males generally reach full skeletal growth at 7 to 8 years of age, adult females at about 5 years. The weights of both sexes may continue to increase for another three to four years. Adult males in Alaska commonly range from 150 to 400 pounds, and adult females range from 125 to 250 pounds. Alaska adults stand at least 26 inches at the shoulders and measure about 5

feet from nose to tail. Although black is the most common color phase, the species can vary from brown to blond to almost white, the latter occurring on certain islands off the British Columbia coast. In Alaska, the black color phase is the norm, but brown or cinnamon animals are often seen in the southcentral region and a rare bluish black phase is found along the St. Elias Range. A patch of white hair on the chest is normal.

Compared to humans, black bears are reported in scientific literature to have poor eyesight. They are, however, also said to have color vision and detailed near vision. In addition to excellent hearing, black bears have a highly developed sense of smell and are able to detect carrion more than a mile away.

Despite their normal shuffling gait, black bears can sprint up to 35 miles per hour and are able swimmers. The toes on each foot are recurved, about an inch long, and non-retractable.

Although captive bears have lived about 25 years, bears in the wild do well to live half that long.

ABOVE: *This brown phase black bear pauses from eating near Eagle, Alaska, near where the Yukon River crosses into Canada. These bears in Alaska are often called "cinnamon" bears to avoid confusion with brown/grizzly bears. Cinnamon bears are more common in the Interior than elsewhere in the state. (Tom Soucek)*

LEFT: *Although black bears are considered forest dwellers, they take to the open occasionally. This slope east of Tok hosted some ursine fraternization one June afternoon between this black bear and a another one, not shown. (Lance R. Peck, Picture Library Associates)*

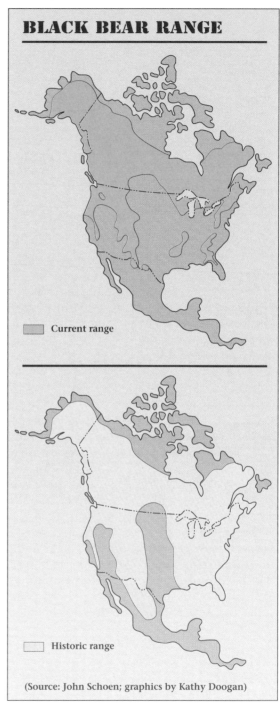

BLACK BEAR RANGE

Current range

Historic range

(Source: John Schoen; graphics by Kathy Doogan)

DISTRIBUTION

Black bears are the most common and widely distributed bears in North America. Prior to European settlement, they inhabited the extensive forested areas of the continent, including Mexico. In many midwestern, eastern and southeastern states, black bear habitat has been replaced by human settlement and the animals have either been eliminated or confined to such highly localized and isolated enclaves that their future survival is uncertain. Although their distribution across the continent has declined substantially, black bears are still common in northern New England, New York, the upper Great Lake states, parts of the Appalachians, and the western United States, Canada and Alaska where they may be found throughout most of the forested portions of the state. Parts of Alaska where they are unlikely to be sighted include the North Slope, the Seward Peninsula, some of the larger islands in the Gulf of Alaska — notably Kodiak, Montague, Hinchinbrook and others — and the Alaska Peninsula beyond the area of Lake Iliamna. Southeast Alaska islands that lack black bear populations include Admiralty, Baranof, Chichagof and Kruzof.

Population densities vary with habitat quality — particularly the availability of food sources. Prince of Wales Island provides a long foraging season and rich food complexes and is known for its historic ability to support comparatively high black bear densities. Black bear densities in parts of interior Alaska are often much lower.

A black bear licks ants from an uprooted tree at Anan Creek. Black bears eat a lot of insects such as field and carpenter ants in spring and summer. (John Hyde)

FOOD

Black bears are opportunistic feeders with relatively inefficient digestive systems, and their diet is determined largely by what is available. Although they are predominantly vegetarian, they eat a variety of plant and

LEFT: Ripe blueberries are a favorite food for both black and brown bears. Backcountry travelers should be particularly cautious when going through berry thickets where bears may be feeding and hard to see. (Cary Anderson)

BELOW: Black bears come in several color variations, including the reddish brown "cinnamon" phase. This cinnamon bear feeds on barnacles in Tracy Arm in southeastern Alaska. (Lynn Schooler)

animal matter. Most mammals, regardless of size, are too swift for bears to catch with consistency, and animal protein is commonly consumed as carrion. Researchers have found that one exception is young moose calves which, on the Kenai Peninsula, have provided a source of spring protein and energy when green plants such as grasses were in short supply. By about the first of July, calves were a month old and able to outrun a pursuing black bear. Although the bears' spring diet of plants consisted primarily of the primitive horsetail or *Equisetum*, grass and sedge, researchers also found them to feed on snowshoe hare, birds and both carpenter and field ants.

In the Kenai Peninsula research, summer diet was transitional between spring and fall in that a larger amount of fruit and berries was consumed and the consumption of green vegetation fell off. The principal summer fruits eaten were the berries of American devil's club and twisted stalk or watermelon berry. Summer consumption of insects, primarily carpenter ants was also high. By fall, bears feeding in previously burned over areas concentrated on lowbush cranberry or devil's club and twisted stalk, depending on which was available.

Black bear feeding habits may be somewhat different during other stages of post-fire plant succession or at other locations in Alaska. Blueberries are, for example, known by biologists and the general public alike to be a common food of black bears. In fact, the perception that bears have become more numerous in an area can often be explained simply by a scarcity of foods such as blueberries that drives bears to search out potential food sources left by people. Occasionally, there will also be reports of cannibalism among black bears.

Not long ago, garbage dumps, like this one near a cannery in Excursion Inlet, were considered good places to watch bears. But bears that frequent dumps can quickly become dangerous pests, having lost their fear of humans by associating people with food. These garbage bears often end up dead, killed in defense of life and property. A number of communities have fenced their dumps and landfills, and a few are baling refuse or building incinerators to cut down on bear problems. (Mark Wayne)

LIFE HISTORY

BEHAVIOR. The degree to which black bears associate with one another depends on the situation. The strongest tie is between a sow and her cubs. Black bears may also congregate around concentrated food sources such as salmon streams or garbage dumps.

Bears use a variety of sounds, gestures and postures to communicate among themselves. When threatening one another or a human, a black bear may lay its ears back and woof or huff, chop its jaws, and, if sufficiently disturbed, stamp its feet. Any of these actions can be accompanied by a charge which in most cases, especially if the object is a human rather than another black bear, may be a bluff. Small cubs "purr" when nursing and let out shrill howls when frightened or otherwise disturbed. A female may make a grunting "uh-uh" sound to call her cubs.

"Bear trees" are those that bears routinely mark by clawing, biting or rubbing — often by males when their hormone levels are highest and they are the most aggressive. Biologists suggest that bear trees provide communication between individuals, but the details of how this might work need further study.

In spite of their tremendous strength, black

bears are remarkably tolerant of humans in most situations. Normally, they will leave an area as a person approaches, and serious encounters can be avoided if people take simple precautions with food and prevent situations where black bears feel threatened. Black bears can adopt nocturnal habits where people become active during daylight hours. Although there are limits as to how much human activity black bears can tolerate, their adaptability has made it possible for them to occupy a broad range of environments that have been altered by humans.

REPRODUCTION AND DENNING. Black bear reproduction is controlled mainly by food abundance, with those feeding on protein-rich food sources showing the greatest weight gains and fertility. Well-nourished females also tend to produce larger, healthier cubs than those that are poorly nourished. In most of North America, adult females first produce cubs at approximately 4 years of age, and males may reach sexual maturity about a year later. It has been suggested that the age of sexual maturity increases at northern latitudes.

Males and females are together briefly

during the summer breeding season. Females remain in estrus throughout the season until they mate. It is common for sows to have young every other year, but they may wait three or four years. Although pregnancy lasts about 220 days, there is what biologists refer to as "delayed implantation." The fertilized eggs are not implanted in the uterus until fall, and actual embryonic development occurs only during the last couple months or so of pregnancy. There are commonly two or three cubs though there can be as many as five.

Born in late January or February while the mother is in hibernation, newborn cubs are naked and blind and weigh only about a half pound. The sow's milk is richer in fat and protein than that of humans or cows, and young cubs grow rapidly, becoming weaned at about six or eight months of age. Sows make good mothers, and cubs den with them during the following winter. Cubs disperse following emergence from the den the second spring, thereby avoiding aggressive males seeking to mate with the sow. The most critical period of a bear's life can be when it gains independence

LEFT: A black bear cub rests in a tree at Anan Creek while its mother fishes for salmon. The sows send their cubs up trees to protect them from bigger bears that sometimes prey on the little ones. The cubs may whine from their perch if they are nervous or lonely. Or the cubs may climb down and run off. The sows become upset when they find their cubs gone. (Pat Costello)

FACING PAGE: A sow and her cub seek dinner at Disappearance Creek on Prince of Wales Island. Gulls await the scraps. (Chip Porter)

at about a year and a half of age. It must finally find food by itself and must avoid the threat of larger bears. During the first year of independence, young bears are generally allowed to share their mother's range. Within

LEFT: Denali State Park in southcentral Alaska is known as black bear country. This handsome specimen is framed by the park's September foliage. (Tom Soucek)

BELOW: People flock each summer to the Anan Creek bear-viewing area, about 30 miles southeast of Wrangell, where as many as 40 black bears gather to feed on pink salmon. Brown bears also feed at the creek, in a rare interaction of the two species. (John Hyde)

another year or two, males generally establish their own elsewhere, and females continue to share part of their mother's range. If the mother dies, it is reported that a daughter will take over her range.

The habit of denning enables bears to occupy a wide range of habitats, including those where winters are harsh and food is scarce for months at a time. Denned bears neither eat nor drink. Excretion of waste is avoided by slowing down the metabolism of protein, the major source of the body's waste products. Small amounts of urine are absorbed by the bladder. Once they emerge from denning, black bears generally eliminate a fecal plug, a wad consisting of vegetation eaten just before hibernation and hair, apparently ingested as the bear licks its coat once in the den. Black bears are often described as hibernating because their body temperature and heart rate fall during denning. Unlike some smaller mammals that can actually be handled without waking from hibernation, bears may awaken when disturbed. To distinguish degrees of hibernation, some biologists prefer to say that bears enter into "winter dormancy."

Denning sites vary considerably, especially at different latitudes. For example, in southern parts of their geographic range, black bears may simply use a nest of grass and leaves on the ground for a den. Other dens are found in brush, cavities of tree roots, rocks and excavations. Piles of fallen trees and the bases of hollow trees are also used. Heavy snow conditions can contribute to the concealment that is important to denning bears. In northern regions especially, dens are commonly lined with leaves, lichens, ferns or rotted wood. Den entrances are commonly closed with leaves or grass, thus retaining warmth and

providing camouflage against intruders.

In Alaska, black bear dens may be found from sea level to alpine areas. During years of abundant food, bears tend to enter dens later than when food is scarce. In northern Mexico, black bears have been reported to den for only a few days or weeks, but Alaska bears commonly den for five to seven months. During unseasonal warm spells, bears may temporarily emerge from their dens. Several days of 50-degree temperatures can be enough to bring them out, but sows with cubs tend to be the last to emerge in the spring.

STATUS OF POPULATIONS

Although accurate population figures are difficult to come by, one author estimated in 1981 that there were probably 175,000 to 225,000 black bears in the United States alone, most of them in the western states. Some publications indicate that in the 1970s, an estimated 25,000 to 30,000 black bears were killed each year in North America.

It is difficult to estimate the number of black bears in Alaska because, as forest dwellers, they cannot be counted reliably through aerial surveys. Although data on bear kills can be used as an index in estimating their total numbers, "sealing" or reporting of black bears by hunting is required in only 14 of the state's 26 Game Management Units. Nevertheless, in a recent brochure published by the Alaska Department of Fish and Game, the U.S. Fish and Wildlife Service, and five other state and federal agencies, the population of black bears in Alaska is estimated at more than 50,000.

Although black bears do not seem to rate as high as brown bears in terms of Alaska's "charismatic megafauna," they are a source of considerable interest among residents and

A black bear rakes its claws on a spruce tree near Sarkar Lake, on northwestern Prince of Wales Island in Southeast. This large, forested island supports high densities of black bears, which are increasingly accessible to hunters through the island's expanding network of logging roads. (Sharon Brosamle)

visitors alike. A growing number of people derive pleasure from viewing them or from simply knowing that they inhabit the same land that people do. Hunting also continues to be a popular use of black bears in the state, and because of the low numbers of young that they produce, bears can be more sensitive to this activity than many other wildlife species. In North America in general, the proportion of a black bear population that can be harvested annually is said to be from 3 to 8 percent, depending on food availability and habitat conditions. In establishing black bear population management objectives by Game Management Unit, the Alaska Department of Fish and Game considers factors such as the desired ratio of males to females in the hunt, the population level that is capable of supporting a given level of bear hunting, and the average skull size of males that are killed by hunters.

Black bears are also killed illegally, and the recent increase in demand for bear parts such as gall bladders, which are presumed to have medicinal powers in other countries, poses a new threat to black bears in North America.

Still other bears are killed when they are thought to be a threat to life or property, such as those which have become habituated to food and garbage improperly disposed of by humans. As Alaska's human population grows, so too does the problem of garbage bears

around communities. For example, Matt Robus, a biologist with the Department of Fish and Game, reports that 15 black bears were killed by police or wildlife biologists in the Juneau area in 1991. They were destroyed because not enough people adequately and consistently secured their garbage. The department reported that during a four-year period between 1987 and 1991, 24 "garbage bears" were destroyed in the community.

Steve Peterson of the Department of Fish and Game sums up the statewide black bear population as "still good." He says there is no indication of black bear numbers drastically falling off. He adds that there are areas where there is considerable black bear hunting and that this sometimes calls for changes in bag limits and season. On Prince of Wales Island, for instance, the establishment of an extensive logging road system has increased physical access to bears. There and elsewhere in Southeast Alaska, the non-resident harvest of black bears has been reduced from two to one in recent years. Other roaded areas of the state where hunter pressure on bears has increased

An alder makes a handy back-scratcher for this black bear shedding its winter coat in Glacier Bay National Park. (John Hyde)

include the Fairbanks area and units on the Kenai Peninsula. Nevertheless, in 17 of the state's 26 Game Management Units, the annual bag limit is a liberal three bears per hunter and the season is year-round. To help ensure hunter success, black bears may also be hunted over bait in designated areas and during specified periods. State hunting regulations require that all bait be biodegradable, and the only parts of fish and game that may be legally used as bait are heads, bones, guts or skin.

Little research has been conducted on the relationships between black bears and their habitats in Southeast Alaska. Black bears have been found to show a preference for clear-cuts on Mitkof Island that were less than 25 years old, where they ate green plants on south-facing clear-cuts in the spring and berries late in the summer and in the fall. Closure of tree tops in the second-growth forest 15 to 25 years following timber harvest significantly reduces food supplies for bears and can limit black bear populations. The availability of den sites may also be reduced in second-growth forests. On Mitkof Island, black bears were found to den in hollow logs or the bases of living and dead hemlocks hollowed out by decay-causing fungi. It may take centuries for trees to attain that size and for their centers to become sufficiently rotten and hollowed out to provide denning sites.

The value of habitat diversity in sustaining black bear and other wildlife populations has long been recognized. Consistent with that concept, it is also necessary to avoid frag-

mentation of habitats that jeopardizes normal behavior essential to bear survival. As Alaska bear biologist John Schoen puts it: "If we are to manage bears successfully over the long-term, we must shift our approach toward understanding their ecological niche rather than simply describing their use of discrete habitat types."

Black bears display considerable mobility in moving between seasonal food sources within their home ranges. In years of food shortage, they may actually go beyond their normal home ranges. There is a need to avoid fragmenting their habitats to the point where this seasonal movement is no longer possible. One of the techniques for minimizing habitat fragmentation in areas of clear-cut timber harvest is known as the "locus method." For illustration, picture a large square block of forest land. The locus method requires logging in a continuous, ever-tightening band beginning on the outside of the block and proceeding in the same direction until its center has been logged. In contrast to the more checkerboardlike clear-cut patterns that are current practice, the locus method maintains the greatest possible amount of contiguous old-growth habitat at any point in time. It also minimizes the amount of forest edge subject to being blown down in high winds and which subjects bears to encounters with humans.

Another habitat management concept involves that of "thresholds" for human activities such as road building or human settlement. Let's say, for example, that if 50 percent of an area is converted from natural habitat to intensive human development or settlement, it is found that a wildlife population in the area ceases to exist. If such an area were divided into two equal parts, with 100

In Petersburg, as in many other towns throughout Alaska, the garbage dump attracts bears. In the 1970s, as many as 30 black bears a day came to feed at the Petersburg dump. The number has dropped in recent years, with conversion to a fenced landfill. Garbage was burned daily until 1989, when the practice was halted for environmental reasons; even so, as shown here, the bears scavenged amid smoke and flames. The city will begin baling garbage in 1994, shipping recyclable materials off the island and burying bales of non-recyclables. A foam will be sprayed over the bales to kill odors that lure bears. In the meantime, residents are trying harder to secure their trash from bears that wander through town. And despite warnings to visitors to stay away from the landfill's garbage bears, "some days, there are more tourists up there than people dumping," said Eli Lucas, public works director. (Don Cornelius)

percent of the land use in one half converted to development or settlement and the other half left entirely alone, the result would be a 50 percent reduction in the total population of the wildlife in the overall area. In actuality, there may be complications such as the effect that the developed area has on the animals in the undeveloped area — perhaps garbage problems in the case of black bears. It is, however, the concept that is important to keep in mind and apply as appropriate in the process of making difficult trade-off decisions regarding land use.

It is after all just such decisions that will determine the degree to which black bears and associated wildlife species will continue to occupy the wide range of habitat conditions that they now do across the state.

BROWN/GRIZZLY BEARS

BY BILL SHERWONIT

Editor's note: *A noted free-lance writer and author of several books, Bill contributes frequently to* ALASKA GEOGRAPHIC®.

Alaska is often called the "last stronghold" of North America's brown/grizzly bears, and for good reason: After more than a century of persecution by humans, this is where *Ursus arctos* has been given its last, best chance to survive.

Based on early records and paleontological finds, researchers believe the species once occupied nearly half the continent. The best guess is that ancestors of modern browns/grizzlies came here about 1.5 million years ago from northeast Asia, across the same Bering Land Bridge.

FACING PAGE: Brown bears exhibit more than a dozen fishing postures, depending on how they were taught as cubs. These two fish for sockeye salmon from their rocky perch at Brooks Falls in Katmai National Park. (Danny Daniels)

Historically, the species ranged from the northern coast of Alaska and western Canada south to Mexico and from the West Coast east across the Great Plains, and perhaps beyond. Grizzly bear fossils have been reported as far east as Ohio and Kentucky.

Tens of thousands of grizzlies may have lived in the Lower 48 as recently as 1850. But the species' range receded and its numbers rapidly declined, as the grizzly came in contact, and conflict, with Euro-American explorers and developers wishing to tame the wilderness and eliminate competitors such as the bear and wolf. Now within the contiguous United States less than 1,000 grizzlies — perhaps as few as 600 — remain, sporadically distributed in isolated groups within Montana, Wyoming, Idaho and Washington. To the north, Canada is home to some 15,000 to 20,000. But the brown/grizzly's primary North American enclave is Alaska. Other brown bear subspecies occupy Europe and Asia with an estimated 100,000 animals in Eurasia.

Past statewide counts of Alaska's brown/grizzlies estimated up to 40,000 bears. Based on recently completed statewide surveys, Department of Fish and Game biologists say their current best guess for Alaska's brown/grizzly population is 31,000 animals. "We're sure we have at least 24,600 animals and probably don't have more than 39,000," says state bear researcher Sterling Miller. "It's important to understand that this doesn't represent a decline. The new numbers are based on better, more refined survey methods. Ultimately it's still guesswork, but now we can make a better guess."

This species occurs throughout nearly the entire state, except for islands of the Aleutian Chain west of Unimak, other islands scattered through Bristol Bay and the Bering Sea and islands south of Frederick Sound in Alaska's Panhandle. And they inhabit nearly every northern ecosystem imaginable, from coastal rain forests to alpine meadows and arctic tundra.

BROWN VS. GRIZZLY

The distinction between Alaska's brown and grizzly bears is rather arbitrary, based more on

An Alaska Peninsula brown bear digs clams on the beach. An estimated 31,000 brown/ grizzly bears live in Alaska, the last North American stronghold for Ursus arctos. *(Tom Soucek)*

Boone & Crockett Club guidelines than scientific evidence. For purposes of big-game trophy classifications, Boone & Crockett established a geographic line that separates brown and grizzly bear populations. In theory, such an artificial border might work nicely; in reality, it can be taken to nonsensical extremes.

"To say that if a bear moves a couple miles and crosses a geographic boundary it goes from being a grizzly to a brown bear is, of course, quite ridiculous," says Larry Aumiller, manager of the state's McNeil River State Game Sanctuary. "There are, however, some general differences between what (wildlife scientists) call grizzlies and brown bears."

In general terms, brown bears are coastal animals while grizzlies occupy interior regions. But whatever their label, members of the species *Ursus arctos* have distinctive body

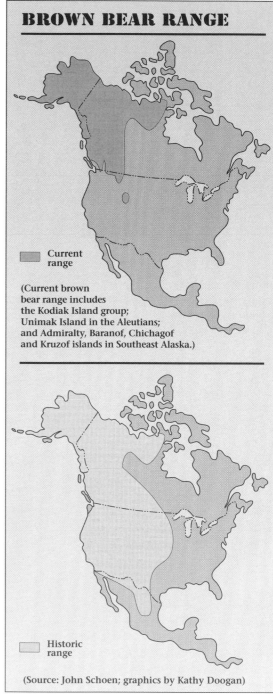

BROWN BEAR RANGE

■ Current range

(Current brown bear range includes the Kodiak Island group; Unimak Island in the Aleutians; and Admiralty, Baranof, Chichagof and Kruzof islands in Southeast Alaska.)

▨ Historic range

(Source: John Schoen; graphics by Kathy Doogan)

shapes, characterized by a large shoulder hump built of fat and muscle; unusually long claws; and a wide, massive head, frequently described as "dish-faced." Their body types have variously been described as chunky, massive, or sturdy, but browns and grizzlies are anything but clumsy. Or slow. They've been clocked at speeds of up to 35 or 40 mph — fast enough to catch a horse — over short distances.

Their fur comes in many colors: brown, cinnamon, red, blond and even black, or a blend of various shades. Many interior bears have hairs with silvery or frosted tips, which gives their fur a "grizzled" appearance.

Like humans, browns and grizzlies are plantigrade animals, which means they can comfortably stand on their hind feet — but only to see better or to feed, not to attack, as commonly portrayed on magazine covers. Also contrary to popular belief, younger members of the species are excellent climbers and even adults can pull themselves several yards up a tree if the limbs are sturdy enough to support their weight.

As with many species, females tend to live longer than males. Biologists have documented females 30 and older, though a sow in her early to mid-20s is an old bear. Males rarely reach their 20s and usually don't survive past their midteens.

Like other bears, grizzlies and browns have a superior sense of smell and excellent hearing. And their eyesight is quite good, despite the popular belief that they have poor vision. Charles Jonkel, a leading bear researcher based in Montana, once said, "I can find you 50 references that say bears have poor vision, but this just isn't so. Perhaps the idea got started because bears do a lot of sniffing when they meet people, in order to check them out. The reason they're sniffing is not because they're

RIGHT: A grizzly cools off in the snow near Toklat River, Denali National Park. (Paul A. Souders)

BELOW: A blond grizzly protects a reindeer carcass (not visible) in the hills inland from Cape Woolley on the Seward Peninsula, about 37 miles northwest of Nome. A few days before this photo was taken, a group of birdwatchers spotted a limping reindeer bull in the small herd that grazed near Cape Woolley. Returning to the area a few days later, the group noted that the bull was missing from the herd and that a trail of reindeer hair indicated a carcass had been drug across the Nome-Teller road and into the hills. The carcass trail led directly to the grizzly patrolling on a slight knoll on the north side of the road. (Penny Rennick)

half blind but because their nose is so tremendously sensitive."

Most researchers also consider the species to be highly intelligent. Sterling Miller explains: "All animals evolve characteristics that enable them to be successful. Humans tend to think through problems, so animals that also seem to do so, we label intelligent. Bears, like humans, show an ability to adapt to a wide variety of circumstances. Like us, they're generalists and opportunists and seem capable of using their intelligence to meet the challenges they face in their lifestyles."

As for the differences between grizzly and brown bears: Grizzlies tend to have longer claws and bigger humps, be lighter colored and have more dish-shaped faces than their coastal cousins. On the average, grizzlies are also considerably smaller animals, largely because brown bears have access to more plentiful energy-rich foods, especially salmon.

Adult female grizzly bears that inhabit the North Slope average about 220 pounds in springtime, says Harry Reynolds, a state biologist who's studied North Slope grizzlies since the early 1970s. Female grizzlies in the Alaska Range average about 280 pounds. Weights are usually taken in spring, when bears are easiest to capture. For purposes of comparison, an adult bear that weighs 220 pounds in the spring may tip the scales at 300 to 350 pounds by the time it enters its den in the fall, Reynolds notes. A large male grizzly may weigh 400 to 500 pounds in spring and 600 to 700 pounds just before denning.

Adult female brown bears average 400 to 500 pounds in early summer, sometimes reaching 600 to 700 pounds in fall. Males, meanwhile, range from 500 to 900 pounds, with some giants reaching weights of 1,200 pounds or more.

Brown bears attain their greatest size on the Kodiak archipelago, which is home to the subspecies *Ursus arctos middendorffi*. All of North America's other brown/grizzly bears belong to the subspecies *Ursus arctos horribilis*. "Differences between the subspecies are pretty subtle," says Vic Barnes, a research biologist with the U.S. Fish and Wildlife Service. "Mainly it has to do with skull features. The skulls of Kodiak bears tend to be wider, a little more massive; that's why so many brown bear

LEFT: These Seward Peninsula grizzlies fed several days on a walrus carcass on a river bank near Solomon, east of Nome. An early spring storm probably washed the dead walrus ashore. (Steve McCutcheon)

FACING PAGE: Many grizzly cubs have these distinctive collar and chest markings in their first summer. The markings fade considerably by the following spring when the cubs are yearlings and are gone completely by the time of young adulthood. The sun bear of Asia wears a similar collar its entire life. (Cliff Riedinger)

A brown bear goes fishing at Brooks Falls, Katmai National Park. (David E. Trask)

larger than females throughout Alaska. Based on movements monitored by radio-collaring techniques, researchers calculated that one Alaska grizzly occupied a remarkable home range of more than 2,000 square miles. Biologists suggest a couple of reasons for the difference between males and females: "Because bears are polygamous, it's to a male's advantage to have a home range that overlaps the home ranges of several females," says Miller. "Plus males have a larger body size, so they may have to roam farther to meet their energy needs."

HOMING INSTINCTS

Because brown/grizzly bears live in overlapping home ranges, they are not considered territorial creatures in the manner of wolves. Yet they do show a strong attachment to their ranges when forcibly removed from familiar grounds. Some individuals have demonstrated a remarkable ability to find their way home. In 1979, state biologists transplanted 47 grizzlies to artificially reduce their numbers in Southcentral Alaska's upper Susitna drainage. A majority of radio-tracked bears eventually returned to their home ranges, in some instances traveling great distances to do so. Bear 237, a 10-year-old male, covered 93 miles in 19 days, while finding his way back. Retransplanted, the bear then traveled 138 miles in 13 days — a trek that included a major river crossing — back to his home range.

Another demonstration of homing instincts was given by a young brown bear in eastern Prince William Sound. Transplanted from

trophies come from Kodiak." Such differences reflect thousands of years of isolation from mainland populations.

No one knows exactly when brown bears first populated the Kodiak chain, but "there's speculation that it happened during the time of Pleistocene glaciation," Barnes says. "It could be that there was some sort of ice bridge, or that the animals got across on ice floes." In any event, Kodiak's browns have evolved into the continent's largest land bears: Its biggest males may weigh up to 1,500 or 1,600 pounds in fall.

Coastal browns also have smaller ranges and live in areas more densely populated by other bears than do grizzlies, again reflecting habitat and food-resource differences. Kodiak, Admiralty Island in Southeast and the Alaska Peninsula's Katmai region all have densities of about one bear per square mile. At the other extreme is the eastern Brooks Range, in Alaska's Arctic, which can sustain only one grizzly for every 35 to 40 square miles.

Home ranges — usually defined as areas that meet all of an individual bear's biologic requirements — show similar variability. On Admiralty Island, for example, females average 10 square miles while on the North Slope they average 130 square miles.

Males' home ranges are two to four times

Cordova, where it had become a nuisance, the 3-year-old male was taken to Montague Island, more than 40 air miles away. Less than a month later, it had returned to the Cordova dump. To do so, it had to swim a minimum of five miles across open water with strong tidal currents.

"When you take a bear and move it, they sometimes show an uncanny ability to find the direction home, and very quickly," Miller says. "How they do this is uncertain, but it's clear they're using something besides landmarks. Perhaps it has to do with magnetite in their brains, which enables them to sense their position relative to the earth's magnetic field. Or maybe they do it by smell somehow, though that seems less likely."

DENNING

Denning, scientists believe, is an adaptive strategy that enables bears to survive prolonged periods of harsh weather in which reduced food supplies, decreased mobility and increased energy requirements combine to make ursine life difficult.

In other words, denning, during the millennia, has proved to be a great way for bears to spend the winter.

The time at which brown/grizzly bears enter and leave their dens varies considerably throughout Alaska, but certain generalities apply in every region. Pregnant females are the first to den and, in the company of newborn

A snowbank at Denali National Park makes a cool climb for these grizzly cubs. Wrestling, playing tag and sliding down snowbanks are some of the ways bears of similar size and status socialize. (Lance R. Peck, Picture Library Associates)

LEFT AND BOTTOM LEFT: A grizzly in the Toklat River, Denali National Park, brings down a caribou wounded earlier by a wolf. She is joined on the kill by her three cubs. (Both by Fred Burris)

cubs, the last to leave their winter shelters, while adult males are the last to den and first to emerge. Somewhere in between are females without young, females with older cubs and adolescents.

At one end of the denning spectrum is Kodiak Island where, in some years, adult males will hibernate for only a month. Or not at all. "Kodiak has pretty moderate weather, so bears tend to stay out as lcng as food is available," says Vic Barnes. Late-autumn salmon runs offer reliable food sources in some drainages until November or December. While Kodiak's males vary their winter pattern from year to year, pregnant females — more dependent on the security of den sites — are more predictable. They usually enter dens by late October or early November and stay there until late May or even June.

Kodiak's wet and mild maritime climate sometimes forces midwinter moves. "We've had some years where bears had to change den sites because of wetness," Barnes says. "I've gone in some (recently abandoned) dens in which the roof was sloughing and there was standing water."

At the other extreme is Alaska's Arctic, where pregnant females may spend up to eight months in dens, from mid-September to late May. Males more typically enter dens in mid-October and leave by mid-May.

In colder regions grizzlies often choose den sites where snow builds up, thus providing additional insulation. "Snow accumulation is a big factor in den location," says University of Alaska Fairbanks bear researcher Fred Dean, who also notes that "the timing of denning seems tied pretty close to heavy snowfall. I've seen significant dens dug in late August, in response to six-inch snowfall."

Browns/grizzlies most commonly dig their own dens, usually on moderate to steep slopes, often weeks before they go into hibernation. The shelters are built to size, for the most efficient use of body heat, and may consist of both an entry tunnel and denning chamber. Some bears build nests made of grass, willow, shrubs or available vegetation.

Alaska Range grizzlies usually dig fairly shallow dens, with roofs about six inches to a foot thick. "Dens may face just about any direction," Dean says, "and they're built at a wide range of elevations. Some are close to river beds, in cut banks, and others are high in the mountains. Frequently they're dug among clumps of willows, perhaps because the roots help to stabilize the den." In Southeast, meanwhile, brown bears seem to prefer old-growth forest; sites are commonly excavated under live trees or snags.

Though dirt dens are preferred throughout most of Alaska, brown bears often use natural rock cavities on both Kodiak and Admiralty islands, where snow insulation is less important because of relatively mild winters.

Inside the den, bears enter a state of dormancy, commonly referred to as hibernation, in which their respiration and heartbeat rates are dramatically reduced. Body

Brown bear siblings play in Brooks River at Katmai National Park. Siblings may stay together a season or two after being weaned. (Greg Syverson)

temperature, however, drops only a few degrees. Bears do not eat, drink, defecate or urinate throughout this period; they survive by living off fat reserves built up during the summer and fall.

THE FIRST YEAR

All of Alaska's brown/grizzly bears begin their life in protected dens, sometime in January or February.

Pregnant females give birth to between one

and four cubs, most commonly two. Naked, blind, toothless and helpless, the cubs weigh less than 1 pound, small enough to fit into a human's cupped hands. They begin nursing almost immediately and nourished by rich milk, the cubs grow quickly. Leaving their den in spring, they'll weigh about 15 pounds. The rapid weight gain will continue through summer and fall; first-year cubs may weigh up to 60 or 70 pounds when they den up for their second winter.

Females with newborn cubs, or cubs of the year as biologists commonly call them, are the last to leave their dens, usually sometime in May or June. Because the young are highly vulnerable, and because adult brown/grizzly bears sometimes practice cannibalism, such families usually spend their first weeks in out-of-the-way, protected places with good visibility, such as upper ridges. "They tend to occupy marginal habitat, where other bears are unlikely to be," says Fred Dean.

Like other members of the species, the new mothers go through a transitional "walking hibernation" phase, characterized by lethargy and poor appetites. During this period, which may last up to a week or more, the bears internally shift gears as they readjust from their wintertime torpor into a highly active summertime mode.

While it takes several days for females to work up an appetite, first-year cubs have frequent hunger pains. And for nutrition, they rely heavily on mother's milk, especially for their first few months outside the den. Spring cubs nurse every two to three hours, initiating

These yearlings at Brooks Falls demonstrate that brown bears can indeed climb trees. (Tom Soucek)

the process by signaling their desire for food. "The nursing vocalization is similar to their distress call," says Larry Aumiller. "It's a short, staccato bleat that rises in volume and rapidity as the levels of distress or need rise."

Based on thousands of hours spent watching McNeil's bears, Aumiller believes that mothers teach their young by example, though he suspects that many of a bear's survival skills are innate. "I've seen cases of abandoned spring cubs, doing the right thing, like fishing for salmon, before they had much of a chance to learn techniques. They're usually pretty inept at it, but they seem to know what to do."

Still, being new to the world and its myriad hazards, first-year cubs are "absolutely dependent on mom," Aumiller says. "She's very

ABOVE: A spring cub catches a ride with his mother across Dog Salmon Creek on Kodiak Island. (Valeria Menke)

RIGHT: Brown bear triplets mimic their mother on the lookout for danger at Brooks River, Katmai National Park. (Geoff and Heidi Garner/Blue Mist Photography)

keyed into them, and they to her." Exactly how cubs key in to their mothers isn't clear. Unlike adults, newborn cubs don't seem to have a well-developed sense of smell. Visual and auditory signals may, in fact, be more crucial to their bonding process. Certainly females use vocalizations, such as "woofing," to call their

cubs when they've become separated.

Perhaps because of bonding limitations, separations between mother and young can in rare instances lead to a peculiar phenomenon known as cub adoption or cub swapping. Such adoptions have been observed at McNeil River, on the Alaska Peninsula, where dozens of bears congregate each summer to feed on salmon. Cubs that wander off and become separated from their mothers (usually while mom is busy fishing) occasionally join up with other family groups. Aumiller, who's witnessed a handful of cub swappings since 1976, says such adoptions result from the unique circumstances of family groups fishing side by side.

A Kodiak brown bear sow with four cubs (one not visible) watches another sow with two yearlings head down O'Malley River on Kodiak Island. Bears will fiercely defend their young when threatened. (David Menke)

They're usually short term, lasting from a few minutes to several hours; but in one case, an adopted cub remained with its new family for an entire season.

"Cubs can get real confused," Aumiller says. "If a cub is fooled into thinking a different female is its mother, the new 'mom' will always take it in. As long as the cub accepts the new situation, it seems to work fine. But if the cub somehow recognizes the other female isn't mom and begins to freak out, it will elicit a very non-maternal, aggressive response. I've seen

a couple situations where cubs got mixed up, went to the wrong female and the non-mom ending up killing (the cubs)."

Adult bears — whether male or female — pose the greatest threat to cubs of the year. Anywhere from 20 percent to 60 percent of first-year cubs die, though a 30- to 40-percent mortality rate is considered the norm. The large majority of those will be killed by other brown/grizzly bears.

Researchers have traditionally theorized that adult males are responsible for most, if not all,

cub killings, though direct observations of such infanticide are rare. The most common speculation is that the loss of nursing cubs triggers the female's estrus cycle, thus providing a breeding opportunity for the male. In recent years, however, there's been increased evidence — most of it coming from McNeil sanctuary — that adult females also prey on cubs.

During the 1980s and early '90s, Larry Aumiller and another Department of Fish and Game employee, Pauline Hessing, witnessed six cases of cubs being killed by other bears — and three of those involved females. Only once was a male clearly identified and on two occasions, cubs were killed by adults of unknown sex.

Aside from predation, researchers believe that accidental deaths such as falls and drownings, disease and malnutrition are significant causes of cub mortality. Some of the larger litters, those with three or four cubs, "might have runts that are just not able to keep up with the rest," says Vic Barnes. "Some might very well die right in the den."

Those grizzlies and browns that survive their first year have a good chance of reaching adulthood, as mortality rates drop dramatically after the first year, to as low as 5 percent to 10 percent. The next major hurdle is weaning, when adolescents are driven away to fend for themselves.

WEANING

Young bears are generally weaned from their mothers during their third summer, at age 2 1/2, though some are kept an additional year. Rarely, females will keep offspring until the start of their fifth summer, as has been documented on Kodiak Island. At the other extreme are cubs weaned at age 1 1/2.

The weaning process is not fully under-

stood, but it appears "there's a hormonal shift in the female that's related to the cessation of lactation," says Aumiller. "The female just flat out quits being a mom; her whole demeanor radically changes. It can happen really quickly, over the period of a day."

A couple years ago at McNeil, Aumiller watched as one of the sanctuary's well-known females suddenly turned on her pair of 2 1/2-year-old cubs. "All of a sudden, she lunged at them," he recalls. "They were really befuddled." During the next two days, the sow became more and more aggressive, chasing the cubs and even biting them on the rumps. Finally, the two cubs "figured out mom didn't want them any more," and left. In less than a week, the female went into estrus and mated.

Cubs usually stay with their mothers in Alaska until their third summer, when they are weaned in often sudden rejection. Here, a grizzly sow in Denali National Park chases away her cub. Soon the cub will accept its independence and go off on its own.
(Cliff Riedinger)

After weaning, siblings may remain together for a season or two, sometimes even denning together. But as they approach maturity, they inevitably part company.

Female offspring tend to establish home ranges that overlap, or are adjacent to, their mother's. Males, however, are likely to wander far in search of new stomping grounds. "Male (adolescents) don't hang around long. They

move out, travel widely," says Harry Reynolds. "They're like teenagers. They like to try things out, get into trouble. And the more they move out of an area they know, the more likely they are to blunder into trouble. Which is one reason males tend to have a higher mortality."

BEHAVIOR

Brown/grizzly bears have long been considered solitary creatures, living in isolation from each other except during the mating season. But in recent years, that simplistic notion has been changing.

Females, for example, spend much of their lives in family units, with a succession of offspring. Siblings may spend one or more seasons in each other's company even after weaning. Cubs, adolescents, and even adults occasionally, demonstrate play behavior. And members of the species sometimes come together in large groups to feed on concentrated food supplies.

Both males and females are polygamous, breeding with several partners during their lifetime, or even in a single season. The age of a female's first breeding may vary from 5 to more than 10 years old. "Coupled" bears may remain together anywhere from a few days to

FACING PAGE: Two brown bears meet in a territorial dispute at McNeil Falls, in McNeil River State Game Sanctuary. Most such disputes are settled without physical harm to either bear. (Bill Sherwonit)

RIGHT: A grizzly cub runs through the fall colors at Denali National Park. Bears, like humans, hit the ground with their entire foot in contrast to dogs, which use only their toes. (Craig Brandt)

a week or more. After a successful mating, females do not immediately become pregnant; through a process known as "delayed implantation" — an adaptation to the species' hibernation lifestyle — the fertilized egg floats in the female's womb for several months. If the female has gained enough weight by the time it enters a den in the fall, the egg will attach to the uterine wall and develop while she is in winter dormancy.

Because mating is a biological necessity, play behavior is perhaps a better indicator of bears' social nature. Based on his many years of observing McNeil sanctuary's brown bears, Aumiller says, "Almost any bear will play. I've even seen 20-plus-year-old males playing, though that's pretty rare. And I've seen a female with spring cubs (temporarily) abandon her cubs to go off and play with an old buddy.

"To get into the play mode, playmates generally have to be of about equal status. An exception to that rule would be moms and their cubs, but even moms tend to be more

ABOVE: A juvenile brown bear climbed several feet up this tree at McNeil River State Game Sanctuary before deciding to give up and come down. The young bear and the eagle were aware of each other, but whether the bear intended to raid the nest is open to speculation. (John W. Warden)

RIGHT: Ground squirrels, such as this one in Denali National Park, are an important food for grizzlies in spring and fall. (Craig Brandt)

passive, because of the size difference."

Among the play activities observed by Aumiller and other researchers are wrestling and other rough-housing, playing tag or chasing each other in circles, playing with sticks or rocks and sliding down snowbanks.

Social interactions are most obvious among female-cub family units but even adult males, which lead a more unsociable lifestyle, share their overlapping ranges with other bears and, in some instances, participate in group "feeds," as at salmon streams or garbage dumps.

When bears congregate, a social hierarchy

inevitably develops with dominance based largely on size. As Aumiller says, "In the world of bears, bigger is definitely better."

There are, of course, exceptions to the rule. For instance, even the largest males tend to avoid confrontations with females that have cubs. Fueled by maternal instincts, such sows are often extremely aggressive. Some, if necessary, will fight to the death to protect their offspring.

Tension often builds in group settings, with stress signaled in a number of ways: yawning, heavy salivation, laid-back ears, body posture, vocalizations such as growls or huffing and deliberate movements. As a rule, the slower the movement of one bear around another, the higher the tension level. Yet only rarely do encounters between stressed-out bears result in fights; less dominant bears are usually given an opportunity to back away. When turf battles do occur, they're usually between bears of equal dominance, with neither willing to back down.

One final aspect of bear behavior merits discussion, their alleged unpredictability. Says Aumiller, "The unpredictability tag is largely tied to the fight or flight question. If encountered (by a human), will they charge, or will they flee? Yet even that, to a certain degree, is predictable; but it requires an understanding of bear behavior. Just like a human, a bear's response depends on many factors: How close are you? What's your behavior? What's the bear's mood?

"In many, many other areas, bears are perfectly predictable. For example, a little bear is going to defer to a big bear. And bears will respond to a food source, whether it's salmon or garbage. In the extreme, if you believe that a bear's behavior is totally unpredictable, a result of random choice, then it doesn't really

Dall sheep near Sable Pass in Denali National Park move to higher pasture as curious grizzly cubs approach. The sow continues grazing, uninterested in the sheep which are virtually impossible for bears to catch. The sow was outfitted with a radio collar because she caused trouble with backcountry campers. Denali's wildlife managers monitor such problem bears to minimize their encounters with people, often by closing areas around them to hikers. They also use "adverse conditioning" such as rubber bullets to train problem bears to avoid humans. This bear died of old age and by summer 1993, the park had only one problem bear; it was successfully relocated to the Grizzly Discovery Center in Montana. A group of non-problem bears in the park, ranging west of Wonder Lake and out of sight of the road, wear radio collars for research purposes. (Alissa Crandall)

matter what you do in bear country. But that's not the case. There are, in fact, certain precautions, certain actions a person can take to avoid an attack, based on what we do know of bears' behavior." [For more on bears and humans, see page 71.]

EATING HABITS

Referring to a grizzly's eating habits, John Muir once commented, "to him almost everything is food except granite." An exaggeration, of course, but not far off the mark. Descended from carnivores, grizzly and brown bears have evolved into opportunistic omnivores. They feed on a wide variety of foods; everything from insects and berries to beached whales and human garbage.

Despite a digestive tract that more closely resembles a human's than an ungulate's,

Grizzly bears that live in forested areas with moose sometimes prey on the young ungulates, which are most vulnerable during their first month of life. This mother moose guards her twin calves at Riley Creek in Denali National Park. A bear will rarely attack an adult moose, unless the moose is sick, injured or old. (Cliff Riedinger)

But calves remain highly vulnerable for only a short period; three to four weeks for moose and two to three weeks for caribou. After that, bear predation drops dramatically. As for adult ungulates, "Grizzlies are much less efficient killers," Miller says. "They do occasionally kill adults, but usually there's something wrong with the animal. It's sick, or injured, or old. It's rare that grizzlies will kill healthy adult moose or caribou."

In only one sense are grizzlies and browns picky: They prefer the high-energy, high-protein food sources needed to build up fat reserves for their long winter dormancy. And they need large quantities of them. It's been estimated that adult bears may eat up to 80 or 90 pounds of food per day during their feeding peak, to gain three to six pounds of fat daily. Because the best foods vary both by season and location, browns and grizzlies must be in the right place at the right time to take advantage of the most abundant, highest-energy resources available. Within each of Alaska's major regions, the bears follow predictable feeding patterns as spring gives way to summer and then fall.

On Kodiak Island, for example, brown bears initially focus on vegetation after leaving their dens. Many graze on sedges and other herbaceous plants found in alpine meadows. Others descend to intertidal beaches, to feed

members of *Ursus arctos* feed on enormous quantities of grasses and sedges at certain seasons. But they also have the physical ability and instincts to be a predator. The effectiveness of grizzlies and brown bears as predators of ungulate species is frequently debated within Alaska's wildlife management circles because of the perception that they compete with humans for species like moose, caribou, sheep and deer.

State bear researcher Sterling Miller, who has extensively studied grizzly predation on moose, says, "They can be very effective at catching newborn moose and caribou calves; for the first couple weeks after birth, grizzlies can kill calves with impunity. They're almost casual about it, it takes almost no effort. And they basically ignore the efforts of (moose and caribou) cows to defend their young."

on newly emergent plants or beach lice found in kelp beds. The lice, up to a half-inch long, can be found "hopping all over the place," says Vic Barnes. "I suppose it's the coastal equivalent of feeding on an ant mound." Springtime plants are occasionally supplemented by winter-killed deer or newly born fawns. But as a rule, deer are not a major source of food.

By late June, salmon begin entering Kodiak's streams and most of the island's bears migrate to favorite fishing sites, where they remain through late summer or into the fall. Some, however, stay in alpine areas and continue to graze like cattle, says Barnes. "We've followed some female bears for years and have never seen them eat salmon."

By mid-August, berry crops have begun to ripen and many of Kodiak's browns will shift to a diet of elderberries and salmonberries. Others will mix fish and berries. Fall, meanwhile, presents a mixed bag of berries, salmon, roots and rodents — voles are a favorite — as bears gorge themselves to add the critical fat. Late-fall sockeye runs in some Kodiak streams will provide easy pickings into November.

At the other extreme are northern grizzlies that inhabit the Brooks Range and arctic coastal plain. "When they come out of dens (in May or June) there's little or nothing to eat, except maybe for some winter kills or overwintered bearberries," Harry Reynolds

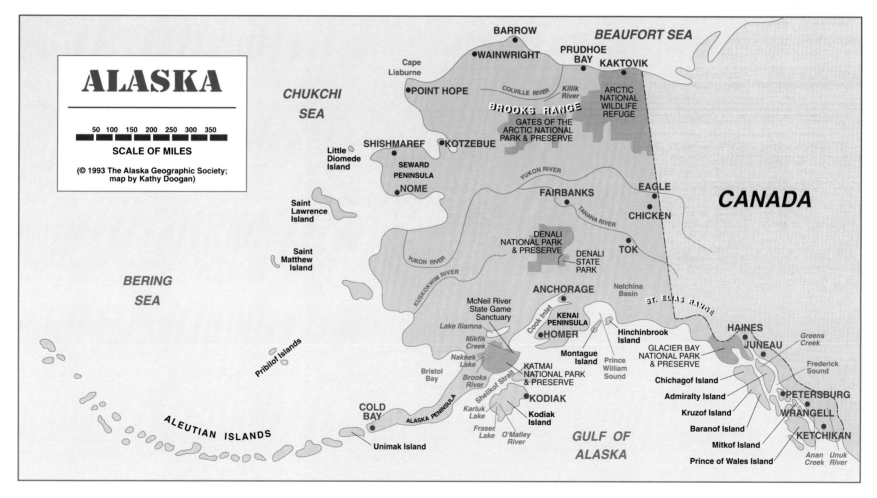

says. "For the most part, they have to live off their fat reserves."

"Green-up" begins in mid-June. From then through July the bears will depend mostly on succulent vegetation such as sedges and Richardson's saxifrage, supplemented by the roots of pea-family plants and a variety of rodents: ground squirrels, mice, voles and lemmings. Caribou calves and less commonly, adults, are occasionally preyed on, but are not a critical ingredient of most bear's diets.

Berries, roots, tubers and rodents are important foods from August into fall with ground squirrels perhaps being most important in terms of calories, Reynolds says. "Some people have hypothesized that the northern limit of ground squirrels determines the northern limits of grizzlies."

THE FUTURE OF BROWN/GRIZZLY BEARS

The brown/grizzly bear, as much as any creature, has come to symbolize North America's shrinking wilderness. Some wildlife experts have called it an indicator species, one whose well-being serves as a measure of an ecosystem's health.

To thrive, and ultimately, to survive, the species requires vast expanses of land where human impact is minimal. Landscapes that humans have chosen to settle or develop have, with few exceptions, historically become uninhabitable for grizzlies and browns, largely because of human intolerance. The Lower 48 is ample proof of that.

Alaska's population of brown/grizzly bears is "basically secure over the next 100 years," Sterling Miller says. "There will be no statewide extirpation of the species over that time." However, he emphasizes, "There are threats to the species."

Among the primary threats is human population growth in rural areas occupied by bears. Such growth inevitably leads to increased defense-of-life-and-property (DLP) kills. A prime example is the Nelchina Basin area in Southcentral Alaska, where in recent years the state made homestead sites available to residents. "Now," says Miller, "people are having bear problems, because they've moved into bear habitat. And they want fewer bears, because they're intolerant."

An even bigger threat, however, is resource development and concomitant habitat loss. "Alaska is a resource-extraction state," Miller says. "And resource development often is very

A grizzly bear chases a wolf in Denali National Park, probably to feed on a caribou that the wolf killed earlier that day. The wolf was seen chasing a group of caribou and then standing guard on something concealed from view. The grizzly suddenly appeared and ran off the wolf. The two animals replayed this scene about seven times during an hour, each time the wolf returned to try and reclaim its kill. (Alissa Crandall)

The grizzly bears of Alaska's Arctic, like this one at Killik River in Gates of the Arctic National Park, cover large territories in their search for food. Some parts of the Arctic support one grizzly for every 35 to 40 square miles compared to Alaska's salmon-rich regions, like Kodiak Island, with a brown bear about every square mile. (Chlaus Lotscher)

hard on wildlife, especially species like the grizzly."

John Schoen, Fish and Game's senior conservation biologist, notes that "Any one development project is not a critical threat. What you have to look at is the cumulative effect. Long-term incremental change to habitat is the biggest concern. At some point you exceed the threshold beyond which bears can exist.

"Most of the Lower 48 problems are waiting on Alaska's doorstep. We're seeing it first in Southeast; bear habitat in some areas is already being compromised by logging and associated activities such as road building."

Another potential problem area is the North Slope, where oil and gas development could eventually result in a major industrial complex that will fragment the habitat.

Development invariably increases human access. And that, in turn, leads to what Schoen calls the "insidious problem" of increased DLP and illegal kills of bears. "Legal hunting can be managed," he says. "That's not the problem. But how do you manage or control illegal kills?"

One key to preserving Alaska's status as the stronghold of the grizzly is to ensure that bears are "very conservatively managed (as a big-game animal)," Miller says. "We still have little technical ability to document population trends. If we err, it should be on the side of caution."

Another key is to maintain large areas where human development is not allowed and hunting is prohibited. Such sanctuaries "are extremely critical," Miller says. "They act as buffers, to ensure protected populations." But even such refuges may not be enough if they become isolated pockets. "Bears need vast areas of wild lands," Schoen says. "We want to avoid a situation where they become isolated and diminished." Schoen also advocates "aggregating impacts. High-density, localized development is preferable to spread-out development. The more we disperse impacts, the greater the cumulative effects." He further recommends that development be kept away from high-density bear-use areas whenever possible. And garbage-disposal methods need to be improved; for example, fuel-fired incinerators are preferable to dumps.

Perhaps most critical of all, land and wildlife managers need to do long-range planning. Five-year or 10-year plans aren't sufficient. "The status of Alaska's bears now and in the immediate future is good," Schoen says. "But we need to be thinking ahead 100 years."

POLAR BEARS

The wild polar bear is the Arctic incarnate. When watching one amble across the pack ice, looking about and periodically sniffing the wind, there is an overwhelming sense that it belongs there. The Arctic is not a forsaken wasteland to a polar bear; it is home, and a comfortable home at that. For thousands of years, the climate, the ice, and the seals upon which it feeds have shaped and finely tuned the evolution of this predator so exquisitely that it has become not just a symbol but the very embodiment of life in the Arctic.
— Canadian polar bear biologist Ian Stirling, in *Polar Bears* (1988)

Great white polar bears, *Ursus maritimus*, roam the frozen north seas and coastal plains of five countries — Canada, Russia, Greenland, Norway's Svalbard region and the United States.

FACING PAGE: Polar bears are the world's largest nonaquatic predators. This 1,400-pound male polar bear roams Alaska's northern Beaufort Sea. (S.C. Amstrup)

Perhaps more than any of Alaska's other bears, these monarchs of the ice inspire respect, awe and fear. They are huge. They eat meat almost exclusively. They spend most of their time on drifting ocean ice, a cold, snowy, windy environment inhospitable to most other forms of life. Yet here polar bears reign supreme. They travel great distances in an almost constant hunt for food. They play, they mate, they teach their young, and they often live to old age. They face few threats, mostly bigger polar bears and humans.

These ice bears, "isbjorn" in Norwegian, are mysterious creatures in many ways. Living as they do at the top of the world, dispersed throughout thousands of square miles of ice, far from most human settlements and in a region with several months of continual darkness, they are not easy animals to observe. For centuries, polar bears have been hunted, killed for meat and furs, and captured alive for emperors and kings. But until relatively recent, little has been known about them in the wild. After nearly 30 years of studying wild polar bears and consulting with Native hunters, who

have a wealth of information from observing the bears of their regions, biologists are getting a clearer picture of where polar bears go, how they spend their time, and what their future may be.

✳ ✳ ✳

Alaska has 3,000 to 5,000 of the world's estimated 40,000 polar bears. They live along Alaska's northern and northwestern coasts, spending most of their time on the ice of the Beaufort, Chukchi and Bering seas. They move with the ice pack, coming as far south as the Pribilof Islands in the eastern Bering Sea. They may come on land fall through spring, when the drift ice meets shore-fast ice. They seem to prefer to stay on drifting ice near leads of open water. During the summer, they range far from land in the high arctic latitudes, probably at the edge of the polar ice cap.

Polar bears are the largest nonaquatic carnivores in the world. The males stand more than 12 feet tall on their hind legs, have a 45-inch neck, leave a 10-inch-wide footprint, and routinely weigh more than half a ton. One of

may boldly approach people out of curiosity, unlike black and brown bears, which usually flee. Polar bears also follow each other's footprints. They do so to scavenge seal kills, prey on smaller bears, find a mate, and possibly because walking in tracks is easier than breaking new trail through the snow. Human footprints resemble bear tracks and probably smell strange and worth investigating.

"The hunter who turns to find a bear walking in his tracks may indeed be in danger. However, he has probably experienced this track-following behavior, rather than an instinct to prey upon humans," writes Steven Amstrup, leader of polar bear research in northern Alaska for U.S. Fish and Wildlife Service, in a 1986 Audubon Wildlife Report. "Polar bears must be respected because of their size, speed and strength. When in the bear's world, humans must take extreme care to stay out of their way."

Early arctic travelers who told of vicious polar bear attacks may have been victims of mistaken identity, suggested Canadian explorer Vilhjalmur Stefansson in 1920. These early explorers ate seal meat, fed seal meat to their dogs, and used seal oil to fuel lights and stoves. They probably smelled just like seals to the bears.

the largest wild polar bears ever handled by researchers in Alaska weighed about 1,600 pounds. Female polar bears are smaller, usually 300 to 700 pounds. The largest brown bears of Kodiak Island and the Alaska Peninsula rival polar bears in size, but these browns are omnivorous, supplementing their diet of salmon with roots, sedges and berries.

Polar bears are true predators. They reach their bulk primarily by feeding on ringed seals. Alaska's polar bears occasionally eat bearded seals, walrus and whales when they can get

them, usually by scavenging carcasses. In a little-understood phenomenon that apparently has more to do with mating behavior than hunger, male polar bears will infrequently kill polar bear cubs. They will also eat polar bear females that die protecting their young.

Polar bears have, on occasion, attacked people. But the sensational characterization of polar bears as marauding killers that deliberately stalk humans is discounted by polar bear experts. Polar bears regularly hunt large animals about the size of humans, and

* * *

Not long ago, a popular notion cast polar bears as circumpolar wanderers, traveling country to country around the top of the globe. This romantic concept of polar nomads began to get some serious attention in the mid-1960s, when the "polar bear nations" began discussing whether an international management plan was needed to protect the animals.

The first international scientific meeting on polar bears convened in Fairbanks in 1965 to talk about this and other concerns, including the dearth of basic knowledge about wild polar bears. "It was a shot in the arm for polar bear research," recalls Jack W. Lentfer, the wildlife biologist in charge of Alaska polar bear management at the time.

In 1967, Lentfer pioneered a program to tranquilize, capture and mark polar bears on the sea ice north of Barrow so they could be tracked to learn where they spend their time. The bears were sedated with tranquilizer darts fired from a helicopter. Working quickly, the researchers tattooed an identification number inside the bears' lip and tagged an ear with the same number. Some bears were numbered on their fur with dye, for short-term aerial observations. While immobilized, researchers weighed and measured the bears and pulled a small deciduous, pre-molar tooth from each to determine its age. Following Lentfer's lead, biologists in Canada and Russia began similar polar bear tagging programs.

Steven Amstrup, U.S. Fish and Wildlife Service polar bear research leader for northern Alaska, weighs a polar bear cub on the Beaufort Sea, part of a study of polar bear ecology in Alaska. (S.C. Amstrup)

In 1972, Congress passed the Marine Mammal Protection Act. Polar bears were covered by the act, and the federal government assumed their management. Lentfer, who had been working for the Alaska Department of Fish and Game, transferred to the U.S. Fish and Wildlife Service and continued his tagging studies. By 1977, he had accumulated a decade of baseline information about the distribution and reproductive biology of Alaska's polar bears. Among other things, he suggested that Alaska had two separate populations of polar bears. With his results compiled, Lentfer went back to work for the state in another capacity.

Meanwhile, Amstrup was working as a research biologist with the U.S. Fish and Wildlife Service in Wyoming. He had been fascinated with bears as long as he could remember. As a child in Minnesota, he had read everything he could about bears, even announcing to his family when he was 5 that he wanted to live with the bears as a forest ranger. Years later as an adult, he found himself among black bears in central Idaho, researching their population and habitat to earn a master's degree in wildlife science. The vacant polar bear research position in Alaska pulled Amstrup like a magnet, and by 1980 he was on the job, seeing these big white mammals for the first time in the wild.

"Each sighting is somewhat similar to the first," he says now, hundreds of bears later. "You catch your breath and think, 'Holy s—, that's a real live polar bear.' They are incredible animals to study."

Amstrup set out to further describe Alaska's polar bear population, its boundaries, and find out where the females denned to have their cubs. He expanded the polar bear tagging program in Alaska. In 1981, he began successfully outfitting polar bears with radio transmitter collars, a new technology that Lentfer had experimented with. Still used today in animal studies, these transmitters emit continuous UHF and VHF signals that can be picked up by aircraft equipped with antennas and receivers.

Then in 1985, Amstrup began using the cutting-edge technology of satellite telemetry. These transmitters monitor the polar bears for movement, body temperature and other vital statistics, bouncing the information off satellites to computers where it is stored until needed. This allowed new insights into some aspects of polar bear ecology. Collaring bears is costly so only a small percentage of bears are monitored. In addition, the expense of tracking them by airplane limits survey flights to five or six a year. Blood samples and claw shavings taken from the bears during tagging

Researchers discovered an unusually large litter of four cubs with this female polar bear near an island offshore of Russia's Chukotsk Peninsula. A radio collar was put on the immobilized female, part of a cooperative field study led by U.S. Fish and Wildlife Service western Alaska polar bear project leader Gerald Garner with Russian researchers. (Scott L. Schliebe, USFWS)

have provided information relating to genetics and environment.

Today, after about 25 years of tracking polar bears, biologists concur that the bears have home territories rather than traveling indiscriminately around the globe. They define about a dozen different groups of polar bears by territorial range. These ranges are vast and may overlap international boundaries.

As Lentfer suspected, Alaska's polar bears form two, mostly separate, populations. Amstrup estimates that about 2,000 polar bears live in the Beaufort Sea, ranging from Point Barrow to Cape Bathurst, Northwest Territories, Canada. Interestingly, these bears seem to observe an invisible boundary, rarely going east of Cape Bathurst into Amundsen Gulf, Amstrup says. Likewise the polar bears of Amundsen Gulf rarely venture west of Cape Bathurst.

The rest of Alaska's polar bears live in the Chukchi and Bering seas to the west. Their range extends from Alaska's coast across to Russia. Amstrup's colleague Gerald Garner has been in charge of research specific to this group since 1986. Western Alaska's polar bears actually spend 60 to 75 percent of their time in Russian territory, Garner says. In April and May, these polar bears move with the receding ice pack out of Alaska's Bering Sea into the north and northwesterly Chukchi Sea, where they remain through summer in Russian territory. Some bears move from the Chukchi Sea into Alaska's western Beaufort Sea, but they ultimately return to the Chukchi Sea, Garner says. In fall and winter when the ice moves down, the western Alaska polar bears range south into the northern Bering Sea, to Saint Lawrence Island and, on occasion, as far south as the Pribilof Islands.

One of the most southerly reportings of an

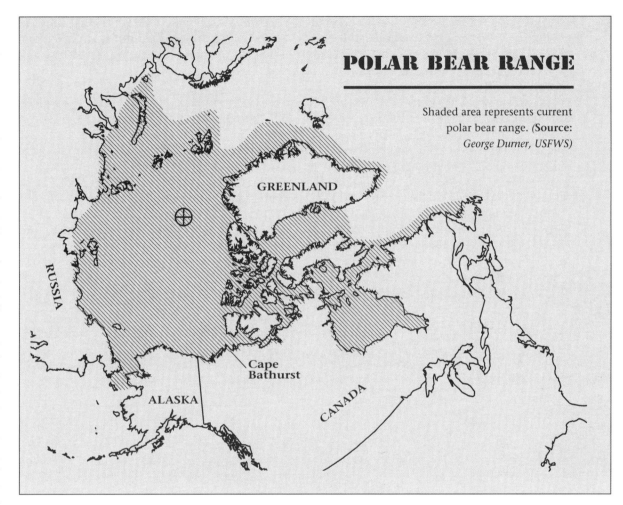

POLAR BEAR RANGE

Shaded area represents current polar bear range. (**Source:** *George Durner, USFWS*)

GREENLAND

RUSSIA

Cape Bathurst

ALASKA

CANADA

Alaska polar bear came in the early 1940s, when a hunting guide reported killing a polar bear on the west side of Kodiak Island. If true, the bear might have followed the ice pack to its southern extreme in the Bering Sea in an unusually cold winter, then traveled hundreds of miles across the Alaska Peninsula and swum across Shelikof Strait. It would have been a rare but not impossible feat given the polar bear's strength and stamina. Biologists know today that northern Alaska's polar bears cover territories averaging more than 95,000 square miles a year. The western Alaska polar bears cover even greater areas because of more active ice, and they average more than 135,000 square miles a year.

One of the big mysteries Amstrup wanted to solve was finding where Alaska's female polar bears went to have their young. There are several well-known polar bear maternity denning areas, including Wrangel Island in the former Soviet Union, the Svalbard archipelago of Norway, and the western coast of Hudson Bay, Canada. No such nursery was known in Alaska.

In the early 1970s with North Slope oil development underway, Lentfer had looked for polar bear maternity dens in the Prudhoe Bay area. They were difficult to spot and few were located. By 1980, only about 35 maternity dens were known, far too few to support the estimated population.

In landmark denning work from 1981 through 1992, Amstrup tagged and tracked female polar bears in the Beaufort Sea. He was surprised to find that about 50 percent of the females routinely denned on drifting pack ice. This contradicted earlier assumptions that polar bears rarely denned on the ice, and did so only when they could not reach land. The remaining females in the study were tracked to dens on the coastal plain, most of them on or near the Arctic National Wildlife Refuge. Amstrup suggests that polar bears are gradually reoccupying land denning areas, reversing a trend begun in the late 1800s when female polar bears using land dens were eliminated by commercial whalers and Native hunters.

The maternity habits of western Alaska polar bears are being revealed through a radio-collaring study started in the mid-1980s, part of a cooperative program between Alaska and Russian researchers. Early on, Lentfer suspected that western Alaska's polar bears den in Russian territory. Radio-collaring supports this assumption. Of 200 female polar bears marked in western Alaska and Russia, all but two have denned in Russia, says Garner, the western Alaska polar bear project leader. Most of the denning takes place on Russia's Wrangel Island.

Two of the females marked in Alaska stayed here to den, Garner said. One denned near Cape Lisburne and the other a short distance east of Barrow. A limited amount of denning takes place in Alaska west of Barrow, he adds. Natives occasionally report seeing mother and cub bear tracks leading from shore to ice. There also is evidence of failed denning attempts. One den on Little Diomede Island was discovered when an Eskimo hunter fell into it and shot the female inside. In March 1992, a young, inexperienced Eskimo hunter killed a female polar bear outside the North Slope village of Wainwright. He led Garner, who was in the village doing research at the time, to the den which contained two healthy cubs. The cubs were sent to the Anchorage zoo, where one died when it fell off a platform in its cage. The other cub was adopted by the Minneapolis zoo.

Unlike the northern Alaska polar bears that den on pack ice, the western Alaska bears apparently do not, Garner says, probably because the Chukchi and Bering sea ice is too active.

Only pregnant female polar bears regularly

Alaska's polar bears depend on a steady diet of ringed seals to survive. This ringed seal has hauled out beside its breathing hole in the ice. Some research suggests that a polar bear needs to kill a ringed seal every five to six days to maintain its body weight. A bear eats the skin and blubber first, to get as many calories as quickly as possible. (S.C. Amstrup)

Although polar bears are not considered aquatic animals, they are strong swimmers, aided by their huge feet that act like oars. This bear was swimming in the Chukchi Sea. (Kathy Frost, ADF&G)

den for extended periods, Amstrup says. The males and other females remain active throughout the year, unlike their brown and black bear cousins that hole up for winter.

Polar bear dens usually consist of one or more chambers dug into deep, compacted snow drifts, connected to the outside by a tunnel. Alaska's female polar bears start having young at age 5. They breed in April and May, but the fertilized eggs do not implant in the uterus and begin growing until about five months later, about the time the females enter dens.

Alaska's polar bears stay in their dens three to six months, during which time their metabolism slows down, with decreased body temperature and heart rates. Although they sleep soundly, they may arouse quickly to defend themselves. Their bodies are exceedingly efficient while hibernating. They complete pregnancy, go through birth, and produce quantities of rich milk to rapidly fatten their cubs. Yet, they do not eat, drink, urinate or defecate. They live off body fat, which breaks down into carbon dioxide and water. The water recirculates through their system. The waste chemical urea, a by-product of protein digestion usually excreted in urine, drops to low levels because they are not eating. Their systems absorb the small amounts of urea that are produced. Some physiologists are studying how bears handle wastes during hibernation, hoping to help humans with kidney problems.

Although males and non-pregnant female polar bears remain active through the winter and do not den, they also experience metabolic slowdowns in what biologists call "walking hibernation." This apparently helps them cope when food is scarce. Researchers doing work with hibernators suspect the metabolic changes are triggered by an opiate-like hormone that enters the bloodstream, possibly in response to colder temperatures or shorter day length, according to David Bruce, a physiologist at Wheaton College, Illinois.

For years, people have argued that bears do not really hibernate. Researchers even adopted the term "carnivorean lethargy" to describe their resting state. The discussion focused on changes in body temperatures. The body temperatures of bears drop only slightly compared to those of "true hibernators," such as ground squirrels and woodchucks, which exhibit plunges in body temperatures to near-freezing levels. This criterion, however, is becoming obsolete. Recent research indicates that body temperatures are a function of surface area to volume; because of this, the larger and better-insulated bears do not cool down as much as the smaller mammals, even though the reductions in their energy needs are about the same. It appears that bears may be "true hibernators" after all.

Back in the dens, the cubs are born in December or January. They are tiny at birth, weighing about a pound-and-a-half. They are most vulnerable during their first two months of life, before they can see or walk.

But the young grow quickly. Mother polar bear milk contains 33 percent milk fat, the richest of any bears and surpassed in the world of mammals only by the milk of seals and certain whales, according to Robert Jenness, a biochemist at the University of Minnesota. The cubs can walk in about five weeks. A few days after they emerge from their dens, after the cubs have had a chance to acclimate to the outside cold, the mothers lead them onto the ice and start teaching them to hunt. By their first fall, the cubs weigh 80 to 200 pounds. They can double their weight during the second year.

In Alaska, cubs stay with their mothers two-and-a-half years. The mothers usually wean their cubs in time to mate in the third year. The long intervals between litters, combined with the late age at which the females reach sexual maturity, give polar bears one of the slowest reproductive rates of any mammal. Theoretically, a female polar bear could produce five litters, since wild polar bears are thought live to about age 20. However, a female in the wild rarely produces that many litters. Bears in zoos often live into their 30s and 40s.

Polar bears have a tremendous sense of smell, and can sniff out their prey from as far away as 30 miles. Seals are malodorous, imparting a strong musky scent to the ice where they haul out. When hunting, a polar bear moves straight toward its prey, pausing occasionally and swinging its head side to side for a better scent. Its short, curved, sharp claws grip the ice, helping it cling to ice floes or climb

ABOVE: A female polar bear guards her new cub on Wrangel Island, Russia, a well-known polar bear denning area. The polar bears of western Alaska move northwesterly toward Russia as the ice recedes in spring, returning to Alaska as the ice advances in fall and winter. Many of western Alaska's pregnant females may stay in Russian territory to den. (Scott L. Schliebe, USFWS)

LEFT: Only pregnant female polar bears den for extended periods of time, to give birth and nurture their cubs. This den was found on Cape Lisburne in northwestern Alaska. A pregnant female needs to gain several hundred pounds of fat before entering the maternity den for up to six months. If she is too lean, she can discontinue the pregnancy and not den, in order to breed again next year. (Kathy Frost, ADF&G)

towering pressure ridges formed when plates of moving ice meet and buckle. The fur covering the soles of its feet provides traction, as well as warmth, against the ice. It can run 35 miles per hour or faster for short distances. It actually paces, moving the legs on the same side of the body in unison.

During a stalk, polar bears may swim across open stretches of water, slipping into the brine to silently glide toward prey. Polar bears can swim for many miles at a time, although they are not considered water-loving animals. Polar bear fur does not repel water, as does that of sea otters and seals, and polar bears can become hypothermic if immersed too long. They do have up to four or five inches of blubber under their fur that insulates them somewhat. Their black skin also absorbs warming ultra-violet rays of sunlight. Another theory holds that their fur acts somewhat like a scuba diver's wet suit, holding water close to the skin to absorb body heat. In any case, a polar bear can swim underwater for about two minutes between breaths, flawlessly navigating through a maze of channels to reach its prey. In an amazing display of athletic power, it can launch itself from the water and land on all four feet on the ice or a seal.

The polar bear's most common hunting method, however, is the "still hunt." In this, the bear waits silently and motionlessly beside a ringed seal's breathing hole. Seals must come up for air periodically and they maintain a series of breathing holes in the ice, scratching them open with the claws of their flippers. They can see shadows of objects on the ice above, and hear sounds of movement amplified through the ice. A polar bear may crouch low or stretch out flat on the ice, to reduce its profile to the seal below. When the seal surfaces to breathe, the bear will grab its head and pull it through the ice. A bear on a still hunt has relentless patience. Alaska photographer Joel Bennett once watched a polar bear stay hunkered down beside a seal's breathing hole for 40 hours.

The idea that a polar bear covers its black nose with a paw while stalking a seal, to more completely camouflage itself, is probably more folklore and cartoon fodder than fact. In his book *Polar Bears* (1988), a well-illustrated, engaging and comprehensive account of the animals, veteran polar bear biologist Ian Stirling attributes the origins of this recurrent legend to an early Danish explorer and a later arctic physiologist in Greenland, who claimed seeing this. Stirling said he never observed such hunting behavior during thousands of hours spent with polar bears off Cape Churchill, Manitoba, Canada. Nor has he ever found a Native hunter who has witnessed it.

When a polar bear makes a kill, it gorges on the choicest fat. It rarely eats the entire seal, usually leaving the kill after about a half-hour perhaps to avoid encountering another,

A polar bear sow and cub walk the beach northeast of Barrow. Up to 30 polar bears roamed town in 1992, after they came ashore to feed on whale carcasses from a bountiful harvest by Eskimo hunters. (Jim Lavrakas, Anchorage Daily News)

possibly larger, bear. A polar bear can eat about 10 percent of its body weight in 30 minutes; the stomach of a large bear can hold about 150 pounds of food.

In the spring, polar bears break into seal birthing lairs to eat seal pups. They stand erect over the lair — a chamber hollowed in the snow on top of the ice — and crash down front feet and head first. If the snow cover is thick and hard, a bear may do this several times before breaking through. Often the mother seal will escape leaving behind its baby. These white-furred young seals do not yet have the blubber needed to survive in the water, and they are not as willing or as quick to leave their warm lair. They are easy prey for bears. They do not provide as much energy for the effort, however, as mature, fatter seals.

In addition to ringed seals, Alaska's polar bears sometimes eat the much larger bearded seals and walrus. However a healthy male walrus can injure a bear with its tusks, and gangs of walruses have been seen chasing polar bears. Amstrup suspects that polar bears feed on walrus more often than reported, particularly in western Alaska where walrus are more abundant. Polar bears also feed on whale carcasses. They congregate at carcasses left by Eskimo bowhead whale hunters. They sometimes wander into villages and

ABOVE: *An adult polar bear hangs in a nylon bag to be weighed in a cooperative study by American and Russian scientists of polar bears of the Chukchi and Bering seas. This bear was on Wrangel Island, Russia. Large bears are weighed on a scale suspended from a helicopter. (Scott L. Schliebe, USFWS)*

RIGHT: *Researcher Steven Amstrup adjusts a satellite collar on a sedated polar bear on the Beaufort Sea. Information collected by recapturing a marked bear, such as this one, during a period of years can be compared to determine growth rates and other details of the animal's life. (S.C. Amstrup)*

✳ THE BEARS OF CHURCHILL ✳

The best known, most photographed and most accessible polar bears to scientists are those of Hudson Bay, Canada. These bears come ashore in late July and August when the sea ice melts. Through the fall until freeze-up around early November, they roam the shores of Ontario and Manitoba where they can be easily seen. Polar bear viewing has become a popular tourist attraction for the town of Churchill, Manitoba, where big-wheeled, high-riding vehicles called "tundra buggies" carry visitors among the bears.

Much of what people know about wild polar bears comes from the many newspaper and magazine articles and television programs about the Churchill bears. But because these bears live in a warmer habitat at the southern edge of polar bear country, they behave differently from the polar bears in the high Arctic, including those in Alaska.

Among other things, these bears are cut off from seals while on land and eat little. Some of them eat kelp from along the shore. Others frequent Churchill's garbage dump. Problem bears are put into cages, or "bear jails," where they are held until the bay freezes. Pregnant females here enter dens before the ice freezes, so they may go eight to nine months with little or no food, living off their fat reserves. These females also reach breeding age a year earlier than Alaska's polar bears, and produce a new litter about every second year instead of every third. Cubs in the Hudson Bay area become self-sufficient and are weaned a year earlier than polar bear cubs in Alaska.

The polar bears of Hudson Bay, Canada, come ashore during late summer when ice in the bay melts. They congregate on land, where they can be easily seen and photographed, until early winter when the bay refreezes. These bears live at the southern limit of polar bear habitat and behave differently from polar bears in Alaska. (Randy Brandon)

One theory is that Alaska cubs need the extra year with their mothers to gain weight needed to break through the thick roofs of seal birthing lairs, an important spring food source.

cause problems, and sometimes they are shot and killed.

In fall 1991, Amstrup witnessed an unusual polar bear feeding frenzy on the ice about 120 miles north of Barter Island. From an airplane, he was trying to track radio-collared female bears to determine the survivorship of their cubs. Many bits of information about adult polar bears come from tracking devices, but the only way to learn about cubs is to watch them. Transmitter collars are never put on the cubs while they are growing.

In a Cessna Conquest flying at high altitude, Amstrup picked up three signals coming from near the same place. This was unusual, he thought, since adult polar bears typically are loners.

For three days working out of Prudhoe Bay, the pilots tried to get Amstrup and another researcher down through the clouds to see what was going on. On the third day, they finally dipped through an opening. They emerged less than a thousand feet above the ice, over an astounding scene. Fourteen bears, including the three collared bears, were gathered around a small hole in the ice where a beluga whale flopped in the water. Strewn about the ice were bloody remains of what appeared to be two other belugas. Apparently the whales had become trapped by ice and had tried to keep a breathing hole open by swimming back and forth. At some point, polar bears gathered and as the whales tired, the bears pulled them from the water. Amstrup had heard of such things happening, but it was the first time he'd ever seen it. "It was impressive, one of the most exciting things I'd seen," he says now.

At the time, there was little chance to marvel. The crew was busy, trying to count bears, record observations, monitor radio

acquired whiter, denser fur that provided better camouflage and warmth. Their long, curved claws previously used for digging roots and catching small mammals became shorter and sharper, better suited for clinging to ice and larger prey. Polar bear cheek teeth acquired sharper, more jagged surfaces for cutting meat, blubber and hide, an improvement over the brown bears' flatter teeth used to grind plants.

For centuries, indigenous people of the polar regions have hunted polar bears for meat and furs. They regarded polar bears as having powerful spirits. The Eskimos of King Island in the Bering Sea considered a polar bear kill to be a man's greatest hunting honor and celebrated the bear's departing spirit with feasting and the Polar Bear Dance, according to a Jesuit priest who observed this ceremony during the late 1930s. The hunter, alone and on foot, not only risked his life killing the bear, he also risked being carried away by the ice, unable to return to land and family. These drifters, as they were called, were considered unlucky or evil, and were to be ignored or killed by villagers who later saw them.

signals. At the same time, they were flying low, making steep turns over rough ice through thickening fog. Nerves were a bit raw. Perhaps some of them were thinking of colleagues John Bevins and George Menkens, who failed to return from a polar bear tracking mission in October 1990. Their plane was last seen on radar about 240 miles northwest of Point Barrow, prime polar bear habitat but far deeper into the polar basin than humans usually venture. After about 15 minutes circling the bears on the beluga, the pilots pulled up above the clouds.

✳ ✳ ✳

Polar bears are among the youngest mammals on earth. They evolved from the ancestors of brown bears between 100,000 years and 250,000 years ago. In captivity, polar bears and brown bears have mated and produced fertile offspring, evidence that the two species are still genetically close.

Perhaps a group of brown bears were cut off from their normal range during one of the late Pleistocene ice ages. They adapted their hunting to kill animals found on the ice. Perhaps the blondest of the bears over time

As shown in this aerial of the Chukchi Sea, Alaska's polar bears are commonly found in areas of active ice, near leads of open water frequented by ringed seals. Pressure ridges, shown at left, are also typical of polar bear habitat. These virtual ice mountains form when sheets of ice collide. These bears are recovering from being tranquilized and marked by Dr. Jim Brooks during early polar bear studies in Alaska. (Steve McCutcheon)

Early on in civilizations far from their arctic range, polar bears reached legendary status. The Pharaohs of ancient Egypt somehow acquired polar bears as pets; hieroglyphics in an ancient tomb show plans for a polar bear burial vault, according to Richard C. Davids in *Lords of the Arctic, a Journey Among Polar Bears* (1982). No one knows how the Egyptians acquired polar bears, although the animals apparently ranged farther south prior to the last ice age based on fossil finds.

Polar bears entertained the Romans, who turned them loose with seals in flooded amphitheaters. Royalty during the Middle Ages in Japan, Norway, Denmark, Germany and England prized the animals as companions, paying great tribute to arctic traders who captured the bears alive. "Polar bears moved around Europe like chess pieces in a game of international diplomacy," writes Davids.

Beginning about 1850, polar bears in Alaska were hunted for their high-value pelts. Among other things, the white pelts made popular backdrops for baby portraits. Through the turn of the century, commercial seal and whale hunters killed many polar bears, apparently wiping out an entire group on St. Matthew Island in the Bering Sea about 1900. In 1874 a sailor who spent nine days on the island reported seeing hundreds of polar bears. These bears were apparently unique in Alaska in that they summered on the island, rather than follow the ice into the high Arctic. Today, all that remains of St. Matthew's polar bears are trails and old bones.

In the early 1940s, hunting of polar bears from airplanes began in Alaska. This shifted the hunting of polar bears from Eskimos using dog sleds taking the animals for food and furs to white sportsmen seeking trophies. Coastal Eskimo families were paid to flesh the hides. By 1965, polar bear hunting was generating about $1,500 per animal, much of it spent in the villages that served as bases for aerial hunting, such as Teller, Kotzebue, Point Hope and Barrow. About 260 polar bears a year, mostly males, were reported killed by sport hunters between 1961 and 1972. Females with cubs were protected from hunting.

Controversy over aerial hunting prompted the state to stop the practice in 1972. But this action came too late to prevent the federal government from assuming polar bear

A mother polar bear sits on the frozen Beaufort Sea with her cubs taking a break from nursing. About half of the female polar bears monitored in northern Alaska give birth on drifting pack ice in the Beaufort Sea. The risks may be greater to bears denning on ice than land, because the ice may break apart destroying the dens, or it may carry the dens far from seals that the bear families need as food when they emerge in the spring. The majority of land-based dens found in northern Alaska are on the coastal plain of the Arctic National Wildlife Refuge, a non-industrialized habitat accessible early in the season because sea ice reaches this part of the coast first. (S.C. Amstrup)

management under the Marine Mammal Protection Act. The act stopped all sport hunting, gave Natives unrestricted access to polar bears for nonwasteful use, and lifted the ban on hunting females and cubs. In 1988, the North Slope Borough of Alaska and the Inuvialuit Game Council of Canada entered a cooperative management agreement that, among other things, asked Native hunters in northern Alaska and northeastern Canada not to shoot cubs or females with cubs.

In recognition of the polar bear's increasing vulnerability to human activities, the five polar bear nations negotiated an International Agreement on the Conservation of Polar Bears in 1973. It prohibited polar bear hunting in areas where they were not traditionally hunted, primarily the high seas of the central arctic basin. It also requested governments to prohibit hunting of females with cubs and in denning areas, to establish controls to prevent illegal trafficking of hides, and to coordinate

LEFT: Polar bear hides taken in subsistence hunting by Inupiat Eskimos of Shishmaref, on Alaska's Seward Peninsula, are stretched to dry. Native Alaskans hunt polar bear for meat and furs; however, the liver contains so much vitamin A it is toxic to humans if eaten. (John W. Warden)

ABOVE: A polar bear's stamina, strength and agility enable it to cover vast distances, traverse towering ice pressure ridges and jump open leads of water. (Lloyd Lowry, ADF&G)

research and management with each other for populations that overlap political boundaries. Polar bear research and management is coordinated internationally by the Polar Bear Specialist Group of the International Union for the Conservation of Nature. Composed of biologists from the polar bear nations, the Polar Bear Group meets every two years.

Each of the polar bear nations has management programs to protect bears and their environment in varying degrees. For instance, Greenland allows only subsistence hunting using traditional, non-motorized means, and cubs and accompanying females are protected. Sport hunting is allowed but strictly controlled in Canada, where most of the North American polar bears are killed. Norway bans killing polar bears in the Svalbard region except in the defense of life and property. In the former Soviet Union, where half the world's polar bear habitat is located, polar bear hunting has been banned since 1955; however the government in 1993 was considering allowing it to start again. This decision could affect the polar bears that move between Alaska and Russia.

Alaska's polar bear numbers appear to have increased during the last 25 years. Yet they remain at risk, say experts like Amstrup and Lentfer, who, in his retirement, serves on the federal Marine Mammal Commission. The population is small, and the bears mature and reproduce slowly. A small margin of safety surrounds any activity affecting the bears or their environment. One of the biggest threats is from hunting; historically, the biggest non-natural killer of polar bears has been bullets. Survival of females is crucial to maintaining the population. Among changes advocated for the Marine Mammal Protection Act, up for renewal in 1993, is one calling for stricter management of subsistence hunting. Amstrup says he has been encouraged, however, by voluntary efforts from Native hunters to reduce hunting of females.

Another highly significant threat to polar bears is arctic industrialization, such as that connected to exploration and development of oil and gas. The influx of people, ships, roads, aircraft and pollution increase potential for bear-human encounters and disturbances to polar bear habitat, food sources and denning areas. Amstrup also wants to look more closely at ringed seal ecology and the interactions between the seals and polar bears, to better understand what is controlling both populations. "Polar bears are vulnerable to any number of disturbances humans cause in the environment," says Amstrup.

"With intensified research and management, most potential conflicts between polar bears and man probably can be resolved. However, the challenges are as immense as the Arctic itself."

A polar bear sow and two cubs from the Beaufort Sea come ashore near Kaktovik on Barter Island. (Marta McWhorter)

BEAR-VIEWING

BY BILL SHERWONIT

ANAN CREEK

Anan Creek is unique among Alaska's bear-viewing areas in that black bears, not brown, are the principal attraction.

Each summer, from early July to mid-August, as many as 30 to 40 black bears gather at this Southeast stream, drawn by a run of more than 100,000 pink salmon.

Even more intriguing, however, is the fact that Anan's black bears share the creek with browns, which they normally tend to avoid.

"It's the only place, really, where you can watch the two species interact," says Dave Rak of the U.S. Forest Service, which manages the Anan Bear Observatory. "You can really see the brown bear's dominance in the way they behave around each other."

Relationships between the two species are

FACING PAGE: Sometimes photographers can get a little carried away in their quest for the perfect wildlife photo. This videographer was a little too up close and personal with an Anan black bear. (Pat Costello)

best observed early in the morning or late at night, when Anan's browns are most likely to fish the creek. They only rarely appear in midday when human presence is greatest. "The brown bears tend to be a lot more secretive," Rak says, "perhaps because of hunting pressure."

The Anan Creek watershed is closed to black bear hunting year-round, but brown bear hunting is allowed within the drainage during fall and spring seasons. Forest Service staff in Wrangell hope that the Alaska Board of Game will enact a brown bear hunting closure, similar to that for blacks, sometime in the near future.

Located about 30 miles southeast of Wrangell in the Tongass National Forest, Anan Creek has been locally known for its summertime gathering of black bears since at least the early 1900s. A viewing platform was built here during the 1930s, but the site received little public attention until the late 1980s. Rak, in fact, describes it as historically a "sleepy little place" that required minimal on-site management.

But as the managers of Pack Creek, about 150 miles to the north, began to restrict visitation at that Admiralty Island bear-viewing site, more people began showing up at Anan. By summer 1989, "we started noting a real deterioration of the trail along the creek," says Rak, who supervises Anan's interpretive staff. "It was clear that the number of people had increased significantly. It was time to get some people on site."

The Forest Service began monitoring human use of Anan Creek in 1990 and counted a much-higher-than-expected 1,200 visitors during the prime viewing period; by 1992, the number had jumped to 1,800. In response, the agency placed a 12-person limit on guided groups. No limits have yet been imposed on private parties, but additional restrictions are likely if visitation continues to grow.

"It only makes common sense," Rak says. "The access trail is crossed in more than a dozen spots by bear trails. We can't have people standing shoulder to shoulder along the trail, because it will hinder the bears' access to and from the creek. I don't think the bears will

BELOW: *Personnel from Tongass National Forest manage the Anan Creek bear-viewing area. Many photographers come here to photograph black and brown bears, although blacks are the most commonly seen species. In 1992 the number of bears seen declined. This trend continued in 1993, and foresters are uncertain of the cause. Managers have speculated that the hot weather of summer 1993 produced an extraordinary crop of blueberries and salmonberries on which bears could feed. Also, hotter weather contributed to lower water levels and fewer salmon in Anan Creek. Increased human visitation may also be a factor, and studies are continuing to find an appropriate balance between bears and humans at Anan. (Michael DeYoung)*

LEFT: *Jeff Stoneman and this black bear share glances at the Anan Creek bear observatory shelter on the mainland southeast of Wrangell. (Michael DeYoung)*

tolerate crowds of people; they'll leave the area if it becomes too congested."

In response to Anan's increased popularity, the Forest Service now stations two-person crews here throughout the July-August bear-viewing period, though visitors are still largely allowed to police themselves. For the most part, the system has worked well. But in 1992 Idaho wildlife photographer-filmmaker Clark Bronson killed one of Anan Creek's brown bear sows, reportedly because the bear had charged him. Bronson eventually pleaded no contest to killing the sow, which had two cubs, in violation of Alaska regulations and was fined $1,500. The cubs were never found and wildlife officials assume they were either killed by other bears or died of starvation.

Also in summer 1992, an abnormally low number of bears were counted at Anan, thus raising the question: Might that population decline reflect the increased human presence?

Though they've kept statistics for only a few years, Forest Service staff have already discovered some interesting facts about Anan's bear-viewing crowd. In 1992, only 17 percent of visitors were from the Wrangell-Ketchikan-Petersburg area; the remaining 83 percent represented 32 states and 15 foreign countries. Thirty-two percent of the bear watchers were guided. And most stayed only 1 1/2 to 2 1/2 hours. Professional photographers, however, averaged seven-hour stays.

The large majority of bear viewers gather at a Forest Service observatory that overlooks Anan Creek Falls. Located about one-half mile from Anan Lagoon, where visitors arrive via plane or boat, the observatory features a log-style wood-frame shelter with two entry ways and several viewing ports.

A half-mile upstream from the observatory is a second, seldom-visited viewing area that remains undeveloped. That site, which overlooks a falls primarily frequented by adult brown bears, is sometimes closed to the public for the safety of both humans and bears.

While most people stay only a couple of hours, Anan Creek does have limited overnight facilities. A Forest Service public-use cabin is located along the shoreline about one mile from the observatory, but it is usually booked solid during the bear-viewing period. Reservations are taken 180 days in advance of use on a first-come, first-served basis. Tent camping is not recommended, both because there's a paucity of appropriate sites and because it increases the chance of human-bear encounters.

For more information on Anan Creek contact the Forest Service's Wrangell Ranger District, P.O. Box 51, Wrangell, 99929 or call (907) 874-2323.

PACK CREEK

To the Tlingit Indians, Admiralty Island in Southeast Alaska is *Kootznoowoo,* "Fortress of the Bears." It's a most appropriate description for one of North America's richest brown bear habitats; about 1,200 of the animals inhabit Admiralty's 1 million acres of coastal rain forest, or nearly one bear for every square mile.

Each summer the island's ursine inhabitants gather at hundreds of clear-water streams to gorge themselves on the five species of Pacific salmon that spawn in Admiralty's waters. The most famous of those salmon streams is Pack Creek, which flows into Seymour Canal on the island's eastern shore.

Other Admiralty streams may support more salmon and attract more bears, but Pack Creek evolved into the island's — and the region's — premier bear-watching site because of its location, accessibility, congregation of highly visible browns and its role as a political bargaining chip back in the 1930s.

Only 25 miles south of Juneau, Pack Creek is a short hop by either plane or boat from Alaska's capital and third-largest city, which makes it an easy-to-reach and relatively inexpensive destination for locals and tourists. From early July to late August, its brown bear crowd is readily observed from either of two designated viewing sites: a sandspit near the creek's mouth and an upstream observation

A few years ago, managers of the Pack Creek bear-viewing area arranged for this tower to be built upstream overlooking the creek itself after the old tower in the background was deemed unsafe. Much of the bear-viewing at Pack Creek is from a spit near the creek's mouth looking into the estuary where the bears feed. (John Hyde, ADF&G)

tower that offers a bird's-eye view of fish and fishers.

As for the influence of politics on Pack Creek's fate: In 1932, the U.S. Congress staged public hearings while considering whether Admiralty Island should be added to the national refuge system. After long and often acrimonious debate, a compromise was finally reached. Admiralty would remain part of Tongass National Forest, but certain areas would be closed to brown bear hunting. One of those was a 20-square-mile block of land around Pack Creek, where bear hunting was officially banned in 1934.

The following year, members of the Civilian Conservation Corps built an elevated viewing

The late Stan Price lived among the brown bears of Pack Creek for nearly four decades. He anchored a floating wanigan along the shore near the Pack Creek estuary, and moved freely among the bears with nothing more than a walking stick. In 1990, the state-owned tidal flats near Pack Creek were designated the Stan Price Wildlife Sanctuary. This photo, taken in 1981, shows Price during an early morning look at the bears. (Bruce H. Baker)

platform in a tree overlooking the creek, to aid bear observations. That tree has since been replaced by a 14-foot-high tower. Built on a gravel bar in the stream, the tower allows users to see about 200 yards up- and downstream.

Decades later, additional protections were afforded to Pack Creek's bears. In 1978, President Jimmy Carter created Admiralty Island National Monument; the unit's Kootznoowoo Wilderness now encompasses 90 percent of Admiralty, thus preserving large tracts of undeveloped coastal rain forest critical to the bear population's well-being. In 1983, the bear-hunting closure around Pack Creek was expanded from 20 to 95 square miles.

Despite Pack Creek's unique niche in Alaska's Panhandle, few people — and most of them locals — came to see its bears until the 1980s.

"Viewing interest was minor prior to the '80s," says Paul Schaefer of the U.S. Forest Service. "But then things just exploded. We went from about 100 people a year in 1980 to roughly 1,000 a year by the end of the decade."

In response to that rapid growth, the Forest Service and Alaska Department of Fish and Game, co-managers of Pack Creek, have enacted a series of restrictions to minimize visitor impacts.

Only 24 people per day are now allowed to visit the site during the prime bear-viewing period, July 10 to Aug. 26. Special visitor-use permits are issued in advance, on a first-come, first-served basis. Made available on March 1, all permits are usually taken by mid-March. Four slots per day are, however, kept open until three days prior to the viewing date, to allow some management flexibility. Good for periods of one to three days, the permits are equally divided among guided and non-guided viewers/photographers.

Viewing hours have been restricted to 9 a.m. to 9 p.m. and viewers' food must be stored and/or eaten at a specifically designated food cache/picnic site. And no camping is permitted in the area except on nearby Windfall Island. Because Windfall and Admiralty are separated by several hundred yards of salt-water, campers need some sort of boat to cross the channel; in 1994, for the first time, a canoe-rental system is scheduled to be in place. Most of Pack Creek's visitors are day-trippers, who fly or boat in from Juneau and do not stay overnight.

All visitors are greeted by either state or federal personnel. Following a short talk on Pack Creek's dos and don'ts, permit-holders are turned loose, says Schaefer, though the options of where to turn are quite limited. Bear-watching is allowed only at the viewing spit or upstream observation tower, which are reached by following designated paths. All other areas are closed to human use.

Pack Creek's managers estimate that up to 25 bears feed on the stream's chum and pink salmon, though it's extremely rare to see more than 10 bears on a given day. The quality of viewing depends largely on the size of the salmon runs, which may vary from several hundred to several thousand fish. "Seeing five to six bears at one time would be a good

viewing day," says Schaefer, who recommends late July and early August as the best time to see large numbers of bears.

One of Pack Creek's notable sidelights is the remnants from Stan Price's former homestead. Price, widely known as the "Bear Man," lived among Pack Creek's bears for more than four decades and was, in his later years, at least partly responsible for the area's growth in popularity. After his death a few years ago, the Alaska Legislature created the Stan Price State Wildlife Sanctuary, which encompasses the state-owned tidelines surrounding Pack Creek.

Pack Creek's managers have used McNeil River State Game Sanctuary as a model in modifying their own bear-viewing system. And like McNeil, Pack Creek has an enviable safety record. Since 1935, says Schaefer, "No one has been injured by a Pack Creek bear, nor have any bears been harmed as a result of the viewing program."

For that sparkling record, he adds, "We give most of the credit to the bears."

For more information about Pack Creek,

Visitors to Pack Creek, near the mouth of Windfall Harbor off Seymour Canal on the east coast of Admiralty Island, focus on the area's large brown bears. Research in the past few years has determined that Admiralty Island has among the world's highest brown bear densities. (John Hyde)

contact the Admiralty Island National Monument office, 8461 Old Dairy Road, Juneau, 99801, or call (907) 586-8790.

O'MALLEY RIVER

Kodiak Island is famous for its abundance of giant brown bears, which along with polar bears are considered among the world's largest land carnivores.

Physically isolated from Alaska's mainland by the Gulf of Alaska and Shelikof Strait, Kodiak's browns have evolved into a separate subspecies (*Ursus arctos middendorffi*). They're distinguished from the rest of North America's brown/grizzly bears (*Ursus arctos horribilis*) by their size and certain skull characteristics. Standing up to 10 feet tall, the biggest of Kodiak's male bears may weigh 1,500 pounds or more.

Not only is Kodiak home to the continent's largest brown bears; it also boasts one of world's highest bear densities. Nearly 3,000 of the animals roam the island, or about one bear for every one to one and one-half square miles. Only Admiralty Island and the Alaska Peninsula's Katmai region have equal or greater densities.

A primary reason for the bear's abundance, and great size, is the seasonal availability of rich salmon runs. At various times throughout the summer and fall, brown bears congregate at streams, lakes and saltwater bays to gorge on sockeyes, silvers, kings, chums and pinks. Popular gathering spots include Ayakulik, Sturgeon, Karluk, O'Malley and Terror rivers, Dog Salmon and Humpy creeks, Karluk, Red and Upper Station lakes and Uyak, Deadman and Sulua bays.

Most of the major feeding areas are within Kodiak National Wildlife Refuge, created in 1941 to protect the island's prime brown bear habitat.

Through most of its first five decades, the refuge had no structured program for those wishing to watch or photograph Kodiak's bears. But visitor-use patterns began changing in the late 1980s; at Kodiak, as at Katmai and Pack Creek, steadily increasing numbers of people were lured by the chance to see brown bears. So in 1990 refuge staff began a trial bear-viewing operation at Dog Salmon Creek near Fraser Lake.

"Our main concern was that people were loving the resource to death. A lot of people had begun visiting certain sites and there was some evidence that they were pushing bears out of the area," says refuge ranger Paul Taylor. "Bears were being adversely impacted by uncontrolled visitation."

The experiment proved successful. More than 40 people participated in the 1990 field test and got to see as many as eight individuals or family groups daily. But because viewing was focused on a salmon-weir site where fish counts are made, it posed certain aesthetic shortcomings. Photographers and videographers weren't thrilled about taking pictures of bears climbing around a fish weir.

In 1992, therefore, the program moved to O'Malley River, a mile-long stream connecting Karluk and O'Malley lakes. There, visitors are

This sow photographed at O'Malley was accompanied by four cubs of the year, an unusual but not unprecedented litter size for Kodiak bears. (David Menke)

taken to a viewing platform that sits atop a knoll. The small wooden deck overlooks a stretch of shallow riffles popular with bears when the sockeye are running, because the fishing is easy.

"It's a more natural setting, a very scenic area," says Taylor, "and there's more bears; O'Malley River has one of the highest summertime concentrations of bears anywhere in the refuge. They wander up and down the riffles, coming and going, working the entire stretch."

Vic Barnes, a research biologist with the U.S. Fish and Wildlife Service, has identified as many as 130 individual bears in the O'Malley area during a single season, including adults and cubs. "It has tremendous potential to be a world-class viewing area," he says.

The O'Malley program runs from early July through mid-September and is centered around two distinct "pulses" of sockeye. The first pulse of fish begins in mid-July and runs through early August; the second occurs in mid-September. During those prime-time periods, visitors may see as many as 40 bears in a day and up to 15 individuals at one time. Bear numbers aren't as great during the mid-August to mid-September lull, but visitors are still likely to see several animals daily.

Most bears seen at O'Malley are adult females, with or without cubs, and adolescents. Very few are adult males, which tend to be quite shy around humans. And for good reason; later in the year, this area will be open to brown bear hunting. And trophy hunters are most interested in Kodiak's large, mature males.

The Kodiak program, patterned after McNeil sanctuary, has tight visitor controls. Only six people per day, always accompanied by a guide, are allowed at the designated viewing

platform. The humans come and go at about the same hour each day to increase their predictability to the bears.

The platform is about a 45-minute walk from a designated campground along Karluk Lake accessible only by floatplane. Facilities include frame-tent structures with bunks and mattresses and a combination storage shed/cook shack.

Kodiak's bear-viewing program was suspended for 1993, after Fish and Wildlife Service officials decided to operate it through a privately owned company. However, Taylor emphasizes, "It's our intent to resume the program in 1994."

Refuge managers expect few changes in the new privately run operation. As in past years, those wishing to visit O'Malley River

LEFT: *Most of the bears visitors see at O'Malley River are females. The large Kodiak male bears are extremely wary of humans because the area is open to hunting at other times of the year and trophy hunters particularly seek the large males. (Harry M. Walker)*

ABOVE: *From a small platform overlooking mile-long O'Malley River, visitors are able to track the comings and goings of some of Kodiak's famed brown bears. Beginning in 1994, this bear-viewing program within Kodiak National Wildlife Refuge will be privately run. (Erwin C. "Bud" Nielsen)*

during the bear-viewing season will have to apply for permits, which are awarded through a random drawing. Successful applicants will then have to pay a special user fee — in the past it has been $100 — to participate.

For more information contact the Kodiak National Wildlife Refuge, 1390 Buskin River Road, Kodiak, Alaska, 99615. The phone number is (907) 497-2600.

BROOKS RIVER

Each July thousands of sockeye, or red, salmon return to the Brooks River, bound for spawning grounds in Brooks Lake.

Yet even as they near the end of their journey, the salmon are faced with one final obstacle. About a mile below Brooks Lake is a 5-foot-high falls. Not high enough to stop the fish, but enough to stall them. At the run's peak, hundreds or even thousands of sockeyes gather below Brooks Falls, awaiting their turn to jump.

Following the salmon to Brooks Falls is the brown bear. During July, it's not unusual to see six, eight, or even a dozen bears at Brooks Falls. Prime fishing sites are occupied by mature males, some weighing a thousand pounds or more, or by sows with cubs to feed. Smaller, less dominant bears hang out on the fringes, often content to wade through pools below the falls or wait for any scraps that float their way.

And following *Ursus arctos* to the falls is *Homo sapiens*.

When the salmon are running and the bears are fishing, people can be found at Brooks Falls from dawn to dusk, stationed on a viewing platform built in 1983 by the National Park Service. In July, that means from about 5 a.m. until nearly midnight.

While only small numbers of die-hard bear-watchers and photographers come early and stay late, large crowds gather daily in late morning and stay through early evening. The platform overflows with visitors from around the world.

So it goes at Brooks Falls through most of July. Lots of fish, lots of bears, lots of people.

Located in Katmai National Park 300 miles southwest of Anchorage, Brooks Falls and nearby Brooks Camp have become one of Alaska's fastest-growing visitor attractions in recent years. The presence of abundant and easy-to-see brown bears puts Brooks in a class with the world's most famous wildlife spectacles. Yet only in the past decade has it become renowned for its bear-viewing.

Built along the one and one-half-mile-long Brooks River that connects Brooks and Naknek lakes, Brooks Camp was the largest of five remote camps established inside Katmai (then a national monument) during the 1940s by Ray Petersen, at that time owner of Northern Consolidated Airlines.

The original camp — later to become Brooks Lodge, now owned and operated by Katmailand, Inc. — consisted of wall tents capable of accommodating up to 30 guests. Nearly all of Petersen's early clients came either to fish or to visit the Valley of 10,000 Smokes.

Back in the camp's early days, visitors saw few bears along the Brooks River despite the area's high bear density — 1.4 bears per square mile according to a recent state and federal study — and easy pickings for sockeye at the falls. Any bears that were observed got chased away by anxious anglers.

A Katmai brownie scrutinizes the waters of Brooks River for a salmon or trout. Thick grass and shrubs along the banks provide cover for the bears during forays along the river. (Michael R. Speaks)

Winding Brooks River connects Brooks Lake with larger Naknek Lake. Feeder streams into Brooks Lake provide excellent spawning areas for salmon, especially red salmon. Each year reds return to Bristol Bay in the world's largest red salmon runs and make their way up the Naknek River, into Naknek Lake, up Brooks River and finally into Brooks Lake and its tributary streams. Many predators greet the fish at each step of their journey. During the peak of the runs in July and August, the salmon must run the gauntlet of Brooks River where the brown bears patrol the river's bank. (Cliff Riedinger)

A dramatic, albeit gradual, change occurred when the Park Service began to actively manage the area in the late 1950s. Within three decades Brooks Camp was transformed from a little-known fishermen's paradise into a world-renowned bear-watcher's haven.

Nowadays, during the peak of the July sockeye run as many as 35 to 40 brown bears inhabit the Brooks River drainage. The bears are best viewed at the falls, but they're also frequently encountered on trails leading to the falls, along the shores of Naknek Lake and near the mouth of the Brooks River, where human fishing is concentrated.

Katmai officials have imposed numerous controls on Brooks Camp visitors to minimize the chances of harmful bear-human encounters, though crowd control hasn't been one of them.

All visitors are given a "welcome to Brooks" bear talk upon their arrival from King Salmon, a small community about 35 miles — or a 20-minute plane ride — away. They're advised of bear-encounter "dos and don'ts," as well as the camp's strictly enforced distance rules:

Humans must remain at least 50 yards from single bears and 100 yards or more from any group of two or more bears except when on viewing platforms.

Although visitors are expected to police themselves, members of the ranger staff regularly patrol Brooks Camp's high-use areas, most notably the lower Brooks River and the Brooks Falls platform.

So far the system has worked almost perfectly. Since the 1960s, only one person has been injured by a bear anywhere in 4-million-acre Katmai National Park. And that injury, which occurred in 1991, was a minor one: A Brooks Camp ranger was bitten on the arm by an aggressive sow with cubs.

In a way, Brooks Camp now offers something of an outdoors zoo experience. Visitors can see wild Alaska brown bears in a controlled and tightly managed environment, without having to leave most civilized amenities behind. The falls viewing platform is only a mile — or about a 20- to 30-minute walk for most people — from the Brooks Camp development, which includes the Park Service's campground and visitor center as well as Katmailand's guest cabins, restrooms, store and main lodge building where day visitors and lodge guests can eat buffet-style meals.

Bear-viewing and backcountry comfort, combined with easy and comparatively cheap bush-plane access, have made Brooks Camp a

LEFT: These visitors to Katmai view one of the park's bears from the safety of one of two viewing platforms overlooking Brooks River. Most visitors to the Brooks River area check in with the rangers at Brooks Camp, then either pitch their tent farther along the shore of Naknek Lake at the official campground, or stay at Brooks Lodge. Brooks River enters the lake just beyond the lodge, and the first of two platforms is just a short walk from the lodge across a floating bridge. The other platform is less than a mile farther upstream and is reached by a trail that branches off the road to the Valley of 10,000 Smokes, another of Katmai's major attractions, and cuts back through the forest to Brooks Falls. (Michael DeYoung)

LOWER LEFT: A brown bear lunges from the bank to chase one of Brooks River's many salmon. Katmai's bears have learned different fishing techniques. Some wait at Brooks Falls for jumping fish to come within reach of their jaws. Others swim with their eyes just below water looking for fish. One large male, known as Diver, has been so successful with this underwater technique that by the end of the fishing season his stomach becomes distended by his prodigious appetite. (Paul A. Souders)

major attraction on the state's summer tourist circuit.

Visitation has grown steadily since the early 1970s. In 1972, the Park Service counted 1,182 recreational visits to Brooks Camp. Twenty years later, the number was 9,283, nearly an eight-fold increase.

Even more dramatic has been Brooks Camp's growing popularity with day trippers, those who fly in and stay several hours, then leave. In 1972 only 47 visitors came to Brooks on day trips. In 1992, a record 6,603 visitors did so — more than 100 times the '72 number.

The public's ever-increasing use of Brooks Camp worries Katmai park officials, who fear that the site's carrying capacity may be exceeded unless limits are placed on visitation. The Park Service has explored several ways of limiting human impact on the site and its ursine inhabitants. Among the options considered: restricting visitor numbers, moving Brooks Camp, or allowing day-use only. A final decision on new visitor restrictions — if any — is expected sometime in 1994.

Because Brooks River remains a popular sport fishing site, angler-bear conflicts have been one of the Park Service's biggest management challenges in recent years. Another is human overcrowding at Brooks Falls. The viewing platform was built to accommodate 25 people, but in July it's often crowded by 30, 40 or even more bear-viewers and photographers.

Recognizing the need for additional viewing space, the Park Service built a second, handicap-accessible platform capable of holding up to 50 people, near the Brooks River's mouth in 1992. Eventually the falls platform will also be enlarged and improved.

The agency's ultimate challenge is to preserve the Brooks experience while refining a unique system that has, for more than a quarter century, allowed bears and humans to peacefully co-exist in close company.

For more information about Brooks Falls and Camp, write to Superintendent, Katmai National Park and Preserve, P.O. Box 7, King Salmon, Alaska, 99613, or call park headquarters at (907) 246-3305. For information about Brooks Lodge, write to Katmailand Inc., 4700 Aircraft Drive, Anchorage, Alaska, 99502; call (800) 544-0551.

MCNEIL RIVER

It's anybody's guess as to how long brown bears have gathered at McNeil Falls. But their presence largely remained a secret until 1954, when *National Geographic* published an article titled "When Giant Alaskan Bears Go Fishing."

Written by Alaska hunter-photographer-naturalist Cecil Rhode, the story described a secluded valley on the Alaska Peninsula where "the largest land-dwelling carnivores gather to feast on a favorite delicacy: live Alaska salmon."

Rhode, who saw up to 32 bears at a time, refrained from giving the site's name or exact location because it was open to brown bear hunting.

Less than a year later, the federal government's territorial Alaska Game Commission closed the McNeil River watershed — located about 200 miles southwest of Anchorage — to brown and grizzly bear hunting. And 12 years after that, the Alaska Legislature established McNeil River State Game Sanctuary "to provide for the permanent protection of brown bear and other wildlife population and their vital habitat in the area of McNeil River."

Because few people visited McNeil through the end of the 1960s, the state established no rules other than the hunting prohibition. But 1970 brought major changes. "We had people running up and down both sides of the river," says Jim Faro, a state biologist who managed McNeil from the late 1960s through the early '70s. "There were even people fishing at the falls, where the bears feed. It was crazy at times. The bears took one look at all the people and left; only a handful remained."

That same summer a McNeil sow was shot and killed by a photography guide, when the bear charged in response to the man's close approach.

BELOW: Three-year-old sister bears Amanda (left) and Kimberly approach bear-watcher Judy Brame at McNeil River. The bruin congregation along the river has been known about for at least 40 years, but not until 1967 did the Alaska Legislature establish the McNeil River State Game Sanctuary. (Alissa Crandall)

RIGHT: Photographers and visitors come from around the world to view McNeil's bears. Visitor permits are selected in a random drawing held by Alaska Department of Fish and Game. Permit applications must be received by March 1 for the 1994 drawing to be held March 15. (John W. Warden)

ABOVE: *As early morning fog rises from Mikfik Creek, this coastal brown bear forages on grasses and sedges. In May and June the bears feed on newly emergent vegetation along the tidal flats before the first runs of salmon appear in the creek. (John W. Warden)*

TOP RIGHT: *In 1988 biologists noted 84 bears feeding at McNeil Falls. There aren't 84 in this photo, but there are enough to impress viewers that when the fish are running, McNeil River is prime brown bear habitat. (Ron Miller)*

Faro realized that tighter controls were necessary, both to prevent future injurious encounters between bears and humans and to bring the bears back to McNeil Falls in greater numbers. Finally, in 1973, the Alaska Board of Game agreed to restrict and regulate human visitors to McNeil sanctuary during the prime-time bear-viewing period in July and August.

Since then, no more than 10 bear-watchers per day — always accompanied by one or two state biologists — have been allowed to visit McNeil Falls.

Because demand is so high, the department conducts an annual drawing to determine permit winners. In 1993, only 280 of 2,147 applicants received permits, and 95 of those were "standbys," which essentially serve as waiting-list permits.

The sanctuary's permit system has been highly successful. Since the state enacted its visitor restrictions, McNeil has evolved into the world's largest gathering of brown bears.

The gathering's focal point is McNeil Falls, where bears come to feed on chum salmon, returning to spawn. During the peak of that July-August chum run, dozens of brown bears congregate. In 1988, biologists identified a record 84 individuals at the falls; including cubs, as many as 106 bears have been observed along the river in a single day. For brown bears to gather in such large numbers and in such close quarters is exceptional.

Even more significant than the number of animals is the fact that no bears have been killed in defense-of-life-and-property, nor have any humans been injured by bears since visitor restrictions were enacted, despite thousands of bear-human encounters, often at close range.

"It's widely assumed that bears and people don't mix," says Larry Aumiller, the sanctuary's manager since 1976. "But here we've shown that they can mix, if you do the right things. To me, that's the most important message of McNeil: humans can co-exist with bears."

Peaceful co-existence is possible because of a simple fact: McNeil's bears are habituated to humans but view them as neutral objects. People do not pose a threat, nor are they a source of food.

To prevent any such association, feeding of bears is forbidden at McNeil as it is throughout Alaska. Furthermore, a designated wood frame building is provided for food storage, cooking and eating. And a no-bears-allowed-in-camp policy is strictly enforced within a well-defined campground area.

To further aid relations between the two species, Aumiller has throughout the years made it easier for bears to read people. The close supervision of sanctuary visitors is, in part, intended to make humans more predictable.

Bears aren't the only ones to receive an education at McNeil, however. This is a valuable learning ground for humans as well.

Many visitors come to McNeil with irrational fears born of ignorance or sensationalized accounts of bear attacks. McNeil helps to change such misconceptions. Visitors discover first-hand that bears aren't man-eating monsters as so often portrayed in literature and news accounts.

Nearly all visitors begin their McNeil experience in Homer, where they hop a floatplane for the one-hour flight across Cook Inlet. On arriving at McNeil, they're directed to a camping area two miles from the falls.

The campground is human turf, but all sanctuary land beyond the campground is the bear zone.

"Out there," Aumiller says, "bears have the right of way."

Until the mid-1980s, few people visited McNeil sanctuary before July 1. With no concentrations of bears to see, there was little reason to. But in 1982, a new pattern began to emerge because of changes at a neighboring stream, Mikfik Creek.

Mikfik is a small, clear-water stream that flows through the sanctuary and enters a saltwater lagoon less than a mile from McNeil River. It hosts a run of sockeye salmon in June, but historically the run has been so small that bears largely ignored the fish. In the early '80s, however, the sockeye return began to increase dramatically for reasons that biologists can only guess. Not surprisingly, increasing numbers of bears have been lured to Mikfik's improved fishing opportunities. And following closely behind the bears have been wildlife watchers and photographers. Increased human visitation to Mikfik Creek prompted the Department of Fish and Game to expand its permit period through most of June, beginning in 1992.

While Mikfik has made the sanctuary's bear-viewing more diverse, McNeil Falls remains the primary focus in July and August.

Located about a mile above McNeil River's mouth, the falls is actually a steplike series of small waterfalls, pools and rapids, stretched along 300 yards of the stream. Individual bears take up fishing positions based on their place in the ursine pecking order.

Longtime on-site manager for the McNeil sanctuary is Larry Aumiller, shown here practicing some bear-human avoidance techniques. According to life-long Alaskan Steve McCutcheon, he, Cecil Rhode and Dick Chace were among the first to urge establishment of a sanctuary for McNeil bears. Cecil Rhode wrote an article about these bears for National Geographic *in 1954. (John W. Warden)*

Prime spots are located along the western bank, opposite the viewing pads. Immediately below the upper falls, the most dominant bears — adult males, some weighing 1,000 pounds or more — jockey for position.

McNeil's bears use a variety of techniques to fish for salmon. Some stand motionless in midstream or along the bank, patiently monitoring the stream. When a chum swims by, they pin it to the stream bottom with their paws, then bite into it. Others use snorkeling techniques and a few even go diving for fish.

Although McNeil is most famous for the large number of bears that fish at the falls, humans who have been here have perhaps an even greater appreciation for the close look they get at members of *Ursus arctos*. It's not uncommon for the most tolerant bears to eat salmon, take naps, or even nurse cubs within 10 to 15 feet of the two viewing pads.

For information about McNeil sanctuary write the Alaska Department of Fish and Game's Division of Wildlife Conservation, 333 Raspberry Road, Anchorage, 99518-1599, or call (907) 267-2179.

BEARS AND HUMANS

BY BILL SHERWONIT

When educating the public about bears, state wildlife biologist Mike McDonald emphasizes anecdotes rather than statistics. But there's one set of numbers he always includes in his talks, to contradict the sensationalized stereotype of bears as marauding, unpredictable killers, lurking in the shadows and waiting to attack.

Here are the numbers, as compiled by the state Division of Public Health and the Department of Fish and Game, and updated through the spring of 1993:

From 1900 through late 1993, there have been only 24 documented cases of people being killed by bears throughout Alaska.

From 1975 through late 1993, at least 29 people have been killed by dogs throughout the state.

FACING PAGE: *Some Katmai bears have learned that fish are sometimes stored in compartments in the floats of floatplanes. With their keen sense of smell, it doesn't take bears long to zero in on fish odors. (Greg Syverson)*

"What we've been raised with is an ingrained fear of bears that's out of proportion to reality," says McDonald, assistant management biologist for the Anchorage area. "Any time there's an attack, it's front-page news."

In addition to overly dramatic and often exploitive bear-mauling accounts, the image of bears as threatening monsters is perpetuated by the covers of many hunting and fishing magazines and the standing, snarling bear mounts displayed in many Alaska public venues.

"This is how we've been taught: If you see a bear, you're gonna get eaten," McDonald says.

The truth is, most bears tend to avoid people whenever possible. Of those humans who do encounter a bear, only a tiny percentage are threatened, much less harmed. And documented cases of bears stalking humans as prey are exceedingly rare.

Still, bears deserve our respect. They are powerful carnivores equipped to kill other large mammals. And when surprised, cornered or otherwise threatened, they will do whatever it takes to remove the perceived threat. That may mean fleeing. Or attacking.

Each spring and summer for the past several years, state biologists have presented numerous bear-awareness clinics to educate people, dispel ursine myths and defuse "bearanoia," which McDonald describes as "excessive fear of bears."

The talks and slide shows are primarily geared to help members of the audience "feel a little more comfortable around bears," McDonald says. He and other biologists do that by exploding many popular myths and providing tips for safe visits to bear country.

One of the most frequently asked questions: Are menstruating women more vulnerable to bear attacks?

A couple of studies have been done on that subject, with mixed results. Back in the late 1970s, University of Montana researcher Bruce Cushing found that polar bears were attracted to menstrual odors. But a 1980s study on black bears by the U.S. Forest Service found that "menstrual odors were essentially ignored by black bears of all ages and either sex, regardless of the season."

The Forest Service researchers felt their findings were of special note because "those are the bears most commonly encountered by campers and hikers." Conversely, few people spend time in the polar bear's world.

To date no similar research has been reported for grizzly/brown bears.

The bottom line, McDonald says, is that "this is another example of something the press has blown out of proportion. As a rule, bears are no more attracted to menstrual odors than they are to perfume or bacon grease. If you burn your tampons away from camp and keep yourself clean, you should be OK."

Because bears have an extraordinary sense of smell and are opportunistic feeders always on the lookout for food, campers are advised to cook all their meals away from tents, to store food away from campsites and to hang food out of reach of bears whenever possible. Bear experts also recommend that anglers remove fishy smelling clothes before entering a tent and store them away from camp. Whenever possible, it's best to avoid any odoriferous foods on backcountry trips, bacon and smoked fish being prime examples.

Garbage, meanwhile, should be stored in an airtight container or burned, with the remains packed out. "Burying garbage just doesn't work," McDonald stresses, "because bears have such great noses and are excellent diggers."

Because most bear attacks occur when a bear feels threatened, backcountry travelers should do what's necessary to avoid sudden and close encounters. "Bears have personal space too, just like people," McDonald says. "You don't want to push it."

Whenever possible, walk in open country during daylight hours. And if you must pass through forested areas or thick brush with limited visibility, make noise. Sing. Talk loudly. Or clap your hands. Some people wear bells or carry portable airhorns, but their effectiveness is debatable.

Keep alert and look for signs of bears, such as fresh tracks, bear scat, claw marks on trees, matted vegetation and animal carcasses. In coastal areas, partly consumed salmon are frequently a sign of recent bear activity. And leave the family dog at home.

Traveling in groups is recommended for a couple of reasons. First, they make more noise, thus reducing the chance of meeting a bear. And they also lessen the likelihood of an attack; no grizzly/brown bear attack has ever been reported on a group of six people or more.

When setting up camp, stay away from trails and berry patches. And avoid areas where scavengers such as ravens have gathered, or which have a rotten smell. A bear's food cache may be nearby, and they often aggressively defend their food supplies. Bears are usually reluctant to leave their cache until it's entirely consumed; they may stay directly on it, or bed nearby, when not feeding.

If a bear is encountered, talk to it. But don't yell. "That might be misinterpreted as

One of the best ways to see grizzlies safely up close is from the free shuttle buses that regularly run on the Denali National Park road. (John W. Warden)

aggression," McDonald explains. "You can also wave your hands, or back away slowly. The important thing is to identify yourself as a human. And for heaven's sake, don't growl!"

And don't run. Running from a bear is, in most instances, the worst possible action because it will almost certainly trigger a bear's predatory instincts. Outrunning a bear is all but impossible, since they've been clocked at up to 35 mph over short distances.

If possible, give the bear an escape route, so it has the option of leaving. And if you're dealing with a female that has cubs, avoid getting between mother and her young.

TOP LEFT: Human garbage, especially improperly handled garbage, is one of the biggest causes of bear-human interaction. More and more Alaska officials are tightening controls on disposal of human garbage in the state. (Randy Brandon)

LEFT: With the window of Brooks Lodge securely covered, a bear pushed in the log wall next to the window to get to 50 pounds of sugar that was inside. (Michael R. Speaks)

ABOVE: This cabin in Fortymile country near Chicken in eastcentral Alaska displays some of the techniques Bush residents use to discourage bears from entering their cabins. (James M. Simmen)

As a general rule, bigger is better with bears. So if there's some way to increase your size, do it. With two or more people, it helps to stand side by side. Or stretch out a piece of clothing, like a jacket or rain poncho.

In a forested area, it might be appropriate to climb a tree. But that brings us to another myth about bears, that grizzlies or browns don't climb trees. In truth, McDonald says, young members of the species are talented tree climbers. And even the older and heavier adults can often pull their way quite high, if a tree has sturdy branches.

Backcountry travelers would also do well to learn bear behavior, so they can determine when a bear is stressed out. When experiencing low-level stress, a bear will often yawn or lightly salivate. As it becomes more agitated, the bear will exhibit various threat displays that in the ursine world are intended to establish dominance without fighting. They include: heavy salivating; huffing, hissing or growling; looking directly at you, sometimes with lowered head or flattened ears; turning sideways to display its size; a stiff-legged walk; slapping its front feet on the ground; swatting vegetation; or jaw popping.

Many threat displays end with the bear

FACING PAGE: This bear at McNeil sanctuary displays some of the initial stress responses that should alert all humans to give way to the bear. Yawning or lightly salivating indicates the bear is under low- level stress; increased salivation, huffing or growling, looking directly at the human, turning sideways to show off its size, a stiff-legged walk, slapping its front feet on the ground, swatting vegetation or jaw popping signify that the bear is under increased stress. (Harry M. Walker)

ABOVE: This brown bear scratches its back on a patch of willows along Mikfik Creek. Bears may stand on their hind legs to get a better scent of any intruder, but they do not attack from that position, unlike portrayals of them in some popular literature. (Tom Soucek)

RIGHT: Karen Cornelius checks out what is left of a food cache at Thin Point Lagoon near Cold Bay on the Alaska Peninsula after bears visited her camp. (Don Cornelius)

walking or running away. But in the extreme, a bear will charge. "If that happens," McDonald says, "what do you do besides wet your pants? No. 1, hold your ground. Basically that tells the animal 'I'm as tough as you, if not tougher.'"

Most charges are, in fact, bluffs. But if a bear makes contact, the best thing to do is fall to the

BELOW: *Now and again construction workers on the trans-Alaska pipeline Haul Road, now called the Dalton Highway, had unorthodox passengers in their pickups. (Charles Kay)*

RIGHT: *Ever-curious brown bear cubs inspect this park service vehicle at Katmai. (Harry M. Walker)*

ground and play dead. Attackees are advised to lie flat on their stomachs, or curl into a ball, hands behind the neck. And remain passive.

"Almost any time a bear charges, it's because the bear feels threatened, not because it's after a meal," McDonald says. "Once the threat is removed, the attack will usually end. Lay there and give the animal a chance to leave. Ease up, slow things down."

There is, however, one situation in which playing dead is not advised: When a bear is behaving like a predator. A hunting bear — one that is treating a human as prey — behaves differently from one that feels

threatened. As explained in a "Safety in Bear Country" manual published by Canada's Northwest Territories Department of Renewable Resources, "A hunting bear does not bother with displays. It may make a direct approach at a fast walk or run, follow you, or circle carefully, making cautious approaches. The bear will show no fear, but rather intense interest."

If you're quite certain that you're being treated as prey, never play dead. Instead, "act aggressively and defend yourself with whatever means available. You want to to appear dominant and frighten the bear. Jump up and

down, shout, wave your arms. Fight back."

Again, such circumstances are exceedingly rare. And usually, at least in daylight hours, they involve black bears.

The possibility of encountering a bear prompts many people to carry a gun when traveling in Alaska's backcountry. The issue of firearm protection, except where prohibited, as in some parks, "becomes a personal choice," McDonald says. But he cautions, "If you choose to carry a weapon, remember that pistols are generally recommended against. The No. 1 thing is to be familiar with the weapon you carry; know how to use it."

The Northwest Territories safety manual further advises: "A firearm used for protection against bears should be powerful, and capable of firing rapid, accurate shots at close range."

There's usually enough fish for all in Katmai's Brooks River, but park officials strictly enforce fishing regulations to prevent bears from associating fish with humans. A violation of those regulations in July 1993 led park rangers to close Brooks River between Brooks Falls and the bridge near the river's mouth to all fishing for more than 10 days in late July and early August. (Michael R. Speaks)

LEFT: *Sometimes hikers can come upon bears unexpectedly, even in open country. A grizzly came upon this trio exploring the Thorofare River valley in Denali National Park. (Cliff Riedinger)*

ABOVE: *Another point to keep in mind in bear country is that bears can blend well with surrounding habitat, as shown by this black bear at Anan Creek. Along Brooks River in Katmai National Park, the grass bordering the trails is so tall by August that hikers on the trail can easily pass within a few feet of a bear hunkered down eating a salmon. (Pat Costello)*

FACING PAGE: *Bear-watchers at Katmai have to follow strict guidelines, staying at least 50 yards from individual bears and 100 yards from groups of two or more except when on the viewing platforms. (Greg Syverson)*

For those with little experience, a short-barrelled, 12-gauge pump shotgun is recommended, in combination with rifled slugs and large buckshot. Another option is a rifle of .30-06 or comparable power, with open or aperture sights."

As a general rule, those unfamiliar with firearm use are more likely to be injured by a gun than a bear. One possible alternative is red-pepper spray, which comes in aerosol cans. The effectiveness of such sprays as bear deterrents is open to debate — they've received mixed reviews from bear experts — but they have nonetheless become quite popular in Alaska in recent years.

Because the canisters sometimes leak, it's best to store the bear sprays in an airtight container. Users are also advised to notify pilots when flying into backcountry areas; if it ever leaked into a cockpit, the spray could disable a pilot and lead to a crash. In fact some air-taxi operations and airlines now prohibit such pepper sprays on their flights.

A handy summary of bear-safety tips is available in a free brochure titled "Bear Facts," cooperatively produced by several state and federal agencies in Alaska. Copies of the brochure can be obtained by contacting: the Alaska Department of Fish and Game, Alaska State Parks, Alaska Division of Fish and Wildlife Protection, Alaska Natural History Association, National Park Service, U.S. Fish and Wildlife Service, U.S. Forest Service, U.S. Bureau of Land Management or the Alaska Public Lands Information Center. Another excellent resource is Stephen Herrero's highly acclaimed book *Bear Attacks: Their Causes and Avoidance* (1985).

LAVERN BEIER:
BROWN BEAR MAN

BY PAT COSTELLO

Editor's note: *Born and raised in Juneau, Pat is a free-lance photographer who specializes in outdoor and wildlife subjects.*

Few have more experience with Southeast Alaska's brown bears than LaVern Beier. As a trapper, big game guide and research technician he has lived among or worked with the big bears for more than half of his 40 years. He is a soft-spoken, unassuming man and except for his bushy, 1880s-era beard there is little to even hint at his reputation as a brown bear expert. But ask him a question about brown bears and there is no doubt. If he doesn't know the answer chances are no one does.

FACING PAGE: LaVern Beier and John Schoen work with a radio-collared brown bear on Admiralty Island. Long-term research in the northern part of the island, prompted by development of the Greens Creek mine, enabled biologists to conclude that Admiralty has among the highest brown bear densities in the world. (John Schoen)

For the past 13 years LaVern has worked as a wildlife technician with the Alaska Department of Fish and Game assisting biologists with studies of brown bear ecology and habitat use in northern Southeast. It is his job to capture, radio-collar and monitor the movement of brown bears. Since he started he has handled almost 300 of the big bears.

Two projects are currently supported by the radio telemetry studies. One, started in 1981, has centered around development of the Greens Creek mine on Admiralty Island and the trends of the brown bear population in that area. Greens Creek operated as the largest silver mine in the world until earlier in 1993 when low silver prices forced a shutdown. Because the study began prior to construction, biologists have had the unprecedented opportunity to study bear populations before, during and after large-scale development. On nearby Chichagof Island the other study focuses on brown bear populations in areas affected by clear-cut logging, associated road-building and increased human access to bear country.

Helicopter capture has proved to be a productive and relatively economic means of collaring bears. The bears use alpine habitat in early summer, where they mate and forage on new vegetation on the steep, green slopes. They are especially active in the evenings and are easy to spot on the open ground and snow fields above tree line. On a good evening in late June it is not unusual for LaVern to see 30 to 40 bears and actually collar up to half a dozen.

"Trouble is, bears don't like helicopters and bears don't like to be herded," says LaVern, hinting at the more exhilarating aspects of a helicopter capture. Success depends on the pilot putting LaVern 30 or 40 feet from the bear for an effective shot with the tranquilizer gun. Once darted, it takes fancy flying to keep the animal away from cliffs or timber where it might be injured or lost. The three to six minutes required for the drug to take effect can be especially interesting. Some bears are fearless and will actually turn and lunge at the helicopter.

In the fall LaVern captures brown bears in snares made of quarter-inch aircraft cable he

ABOVE: As a trapper, big game guide and wildlife research technician, 40-year-old LaVern Beier is at home among the thick forests of northern Southeast. (Pat Costello)

TOP RIGHT: Most of the state's brown bears seem to prefer dens excavated in dirt where they can get maximum snow insulation, but the milder climate of Southeast and Kodiak Island allows bears in these regions to use natural rock cavities like this one shown being inspected by LaVern Beier. (John Schoen)

sets on trails next to salmon-spawning streams. One end of the cable is attached to a large tree or log and the other has a spring-loaded loop that catches a bear by the leg and secures it until LaVern arrives with the tranquilizer gun. "A lot of people think this sounds like high adventure but it's everything but fun. So many things can go wrong. When you approach an aggressive bear you never know if it has been chewing on the cable or has been caught by just two toes."

Whether captured in a foot-hold snare or with the aid of a helicopter the processing routine is the same. Once a bear is immobilized and can be safely approached, LaVern and project biologist Kim Titus go to work. In the 45 minutes to an hour before it wakes up they will measure and weigh the bear, pull a tooth to later determine its age and take a hair sample to test for heavy metals. Finally they attach a numbered tag in the bear's ear and a radio collar around its neck.

Currently 65 bears are wearing active collars, which continue to transmit for up to four years. They are monitored by aerial radio telemetry flights twice weekly over the 540 square miles that comprise both study areas.

This radio telemetry work is the first concerted effort to track Southeast's brown bears and much of what is known about their habits has resulted from these studies. Most bears have a smaller home range than previously believed and "interior" bears have been identified. These individuals remain inland year-round instead of traveling to coastal streams to feed on salmon in the fall.

"Through mark-recapture studies we've determined the population on Admiralty to be one bear per square mile," says LaVern. "When we began some doubted there were enough bears in the study area to support this research but we now know it is one of the most densely populated brown bear areas in the world."

Studies on Chichagof indicate road-building may be more damaging to brown bears than habitat loss because roads provide access and increase bear-human encounters. Hunting can be managed but poaching and defense of life and property killings cannot. Viability of bear populations in these areas may depend on managing access.

LaVern sums up his contribution to this research modestly: "If someone wants to capture a bear I can figure out how much it is going to cost and how we should go about it safely." Despite this matter-of-fact attitude it is obvious that brown bears are more that just a job to LaVern, they are a way of life.

LaVern Beier came to Alaska in 1970 at age 17 for a visit and never left. Soon he'd hooked up with an unlikely trapping partner, 61-year-old Bruce Johnstone, a legendary brown bear man.

Johnstone lived a pioneer lifestyle in the Southeast wilderness and had worked as a bear hunting guide, logger, prospector and trapper. He attained notoriety in 1935 when killed Old Groaner, an exceptionally large, one-eyed

A brown bear on the tidal flats of Admiralty Island chews a mouthful of sedges, one of the first spring foods available to bears. (John Hyde)

LEFT: In spring, many brown bears gather in alpine areas of Admiralty Island to feed on new vegetation and to mate. They are more easily captured in these open meadows where they can be darted and herded with helicopters until the drug immobilizes them. Here LaVern Beier inspects bear 10, a male. (John Schoen)

ABOVE: LaVern Beier fashions bear snares out of quarter-inch aircraft cable. One end of the cable is attached to a large tree or log, the other forms a spring-loaded loop that catches a bear by the leg. (John Schoen)

brown bear whose badly misshapen skull contained five bullets, presumably fired 12 years earlier by an unfortunate trapper who had disappeared without a trace. The bear was known for it's pitiful moaning and groaning — no doubt the result of it's poorly healed wounds and badly ulcerated teeth. Johnstone had been stalked by the bear and finally stopped its charge with three shots at close range.

In 1962 Johnstone had an even more harrowing experience with bears, this time fending off three attackers. He'd been in the wrong place at the wrong time and found himself between a sow, cub and boar. Because of a badly misfiring rifle, he'd literally engaged in hand-to-hand combat with the bears before help arrived. He spent the next two weeks in the hospital, badly mauled. Johnstone was still on crutches when LaVern met him eight years later.

For three seasons they trapped beaver up the Unuk River, often passing the locations of Johnstone's bear attacks. He was articulate and colorful and he often told stories about bears. LaVern credits his interest in bears to Johnstone, "That's where it all started, being around Bruce because bears had been so significant in his life. His bear stories became part of my vocabulary. It just kind of rubbed off."

LaVern's real initiation came in the spring of 1973. While checking some beaver traps he heard a branch snap behind him. Expecting to see a moose, he turned to see instead a large brown bear following his tracks. It charged. LaVern recalls thinking, "Oh my God. It's really happening to me."

He decided there was no choice but to shoot the bear if it crossed a small stream about 20 feet away. It crossed the stream on a run and kept coming. By the time LaVern found the bear in his scope all he could see was its head. The .338 stopped the charge but did not kill the bear. Three shots later the bear was down for good.

"Once you have that kind of experience some people put you in a different kind of light," LaVern says. "They assume you are a bear expert just because you survived."

Hired by the Alaska Department of Fish and Game shortly after his bear incident, he worked initially on salmon weirs but soon found himself trapping nuisance black bears in Petersburg. For three seasons he worked with black bears and learned how to use foot-hold snares and administer tranquilizing drugs properly.

In 1979 LaVern moved north to Juneau and met up with another brown bear man, Master Guide Karl Lane. He spent the next nine years with Lane guiding brown bear hunters each spring on southern Admiralty, Baranof and Chichagof islands.

Karl Lane had been a guide since 1949 and had spent some time as a logger as well. When he became aware of plans to build roads the full-length of Admiralty to support logging, he got involved in efforts that eventually led to preservation of the island as a national monument and wilderness area.

"Karl recognized Admiralty as the jewel of Southeast. He had a reverence for the land and I admired him. He showed me that hunters needed to be conservationists too. I respected that. Just like Bruce, a little bit of Karl rubbed off."

Whether he will admit it or not LaVern Beier is this generation's brown bear man. Alive in him is the legacy of the past and the hope for the future of the Southeast Alaska's brown bears. With luck a little bit of LaVern will rub off on brown bear men yet to come.

BELOW: Biologists use tranquilizer darts, formerly filled with M99 and more recently filled with Telazol, to immobilize brown bears for research. The drugs affect the central nervous system. (Pat Costello)

LEFT: Research technician LaVern Beier darts a brown bear in the alpine country of Admiralty Island. (John Schoen)

ON THE TRAIL OF THE
BROWN BEAR

BY ROGER KAYE

Editor's note: *Roger, of Fairbanks, is a pilot and U.S. Fish and Wildlife Service employee who writes frequently for* ALASKA GEOGRAPHIC®.

Our Cessna rose with the updraft, rolling gracefully where the arctic wind encountered the steep rock face. Its wavering left wing pointed north to the coastal plain of the Arctic National Wildlife Refuge, and beyond to the still frozen Beaufort Sea. The right wing followed the northern side of a Brooks Range foothill, an austere, grey wall sweeping upward for 800 feet or more.

Wildlife biologist Don Young listened to the signal from his radio-telemetry receiver as he searched the passing ravines and scree slopes. Somewhere down there, they hid bear 1516, a blond 4-year-old sow he knew well.

FACING PAGE: John Hechtel (in blue) and Dick Shideler attach a radio collar to this grizzly on the arctic coastal plane west of the Arctic National Wildlife Refuge. (John W. Warden)

A bear researcher with the U.S. Fish and Wildlife Service, Young is studying the ecology and movements of brown bears in areas of the Arctic Refuge that may be impacted by oil exploration and development. This summer he is recapturing radio-collared bears, replacing their aging radios with fresh ones and following their travels with periodic relocation flights. His project seeks to compare the predation risks to the Porcupine caribou herd on its traditional coastal plain calving grounds with areas to which it may be displaced should oil development occur.

THE QUESTION

The welfare of the Porcupine herd, whose annual migration is often described as North America's most spectacular wildlife event, is at the center of a lingering debate over whether the refuge's coastal plain calving ground should be leased for gas and oil development or protected as wilderness. The Alaska National Interest Lands Conservation Act, which doubled the size of the Arctic Refuge, also placed the coastal plain in a study category.

The act called for a full assessment of the refuge's resources and ordered an evaluation of potential environmental impacts of oil development.

"The early baseline studies generated a wealth of general information on the numbers and biology of caribou and bears," Young said. "But now we're more strongly focused on assessing potential impacts on wildlife and habitat and developing mitigation options. This project was designed to answer specific questions about the interrelationships between caribou and predators, particularly bears."

The study's predominate question asks how caribou calf survival will be affected if petroleum related activity on the coastal plain causes pregnant females to move to the foothills where bears are much more numerous.

To answer that question, Young has spent much of the last three summers in small, specially equipped aircraft, radiotracking 66 bears. That's a large sample size, he said, considering there are about 100 or so bears inhabiting the study area. He estimates he has

ABOVE: Don Young uses a centrifuge to separate out various components from samples of bear blood. The blood is later analyzed to determine if the animal has certain diseases, among other things. (Roger Kaye, USFWS)

ABOVE RIGHT: Biologist Don Young uses a computer and sophisticated electronics to track bears wearing radio collars in the Brooks Range. (Roger Kaye, USFWS)

recorded more than 1,000 aerial relocations during the last three field seasons.

This year Young's field season began in May with a recapturing project based out of a lakeside camp within the Franklin Mountains south of the study area. After being located by our small plane, bears were captured by shooting them with a tranquilizer dart fired from a helicopter.

The drug he now uses, Telazol, immobilizes and anesthetizes the bear and has few adverse side effects compared to drugs previously used. "The animals are less stressed, and recover less agitated now," Young said.

When processing bears Young packs a .44 Magnum revolver on his hip, but in handling some 150 grizzly and polar bears, he's never drawn it. "Never had a close call," he said, although admitting that each time he first approaches an immobilized bear, a tinge of anxiety runs through him. "There's always some remote possibility that the drug isn't working correctly," he said. "But overall, there's probably less of a threat from the bear we're working on than others that might be in the area. When we work on a sow, we're always on the lookout for a possessive boyfriend."

Before a research participant like 1516 is fitted with a new collar, it gets a physical exam. First, the bear is rolled onto a net, then hoisted up under a portable tripod with a scale. Measurements of the bear's total length, and neck and chest girth are taken; they will be used to track growth rate. Tooth condition is noted. The animal's lip tattoo, applied during its first capture to provide positive identification, is checked and redone if necessary.

Young does a condition index, running his fingers across the animal's ribs to determine the amount of fat accumulation. "Fat is healthy for bears," Young said. "It's related to their overwinter survival and reproductive success."

Finally, the biologist extracts 40 ccs of blood from a femoral vein. Back in camp, a small centrifuge will separate red blood cells from

Scientists use calipers to measure this brown bear's skull on Kodiak's Aliulik Peninsula. According to researcher Vic Barnes, the skulls of Kodiak bears tend to be wider and more massive than those of other brown bears in Alaska. (Marion Stirrup)

the serum and both components will be sent to a lab to test for brucellosis, infectious canine hepatitis, leptospirosis and other diseases. Sera samples are deposited in the Alaska Wildlife Serum Bank, where frozen at minus 40 degrees C, they will be available for future research.

IN THE FOOTHILLS

Right-left-right-left, my thumb flipped a toggle on the plane's control wheel while my ears compared the strength of the signal received by each wing's antenna. It isn't always easy to find a bear, even if it is wearing a transmitter. The pulsed radio-signal indicated we were close, but we still couldn't see bear 1516. Bears exhibit a variety of responses to the tracking plane. Some run, some hide, some continue their activity with non-chalance.

This hider was a lone female. Young had first captured her in May 1989, about 10 miles north. She was an 85-pound 2-year-old then, still living with her mother, also radio-collared. In July 1991 Young found her mother being eaten by an adult male bear, one that presumably had killed her. Three weeks before this flight Young had recaptured 1516 near the Okerokovik River, just a few miles away. She registered 143 pounds on his scale, some-what lighter than average for a Brooks Range female grizzly.

On the third pass a movement at the base of the slope caught the biologist's eye. "I've got it — she's one o'clock now — running below the ridge."

As the plane closed in, the bear turned

A biologist tattoos this Kodiak brown bear in the groin. (Marion Stirrup)

Alaska Department of Fish and Game officials check a lip tattoo on this bear darted near Prudhoe Bay. (John W. Warden)

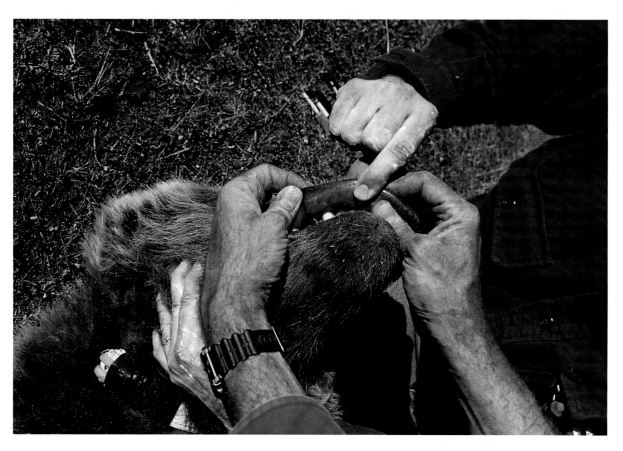

uphill. "She has something...a calf in her mouth," Young said matter-of-factly.

We circled the bear as Young noted the habitat type: rocky slope interspersed with tundra vegetation. He mapped the location and searched to see if any other animals were in proximity. He recorded a group of about 20 caribou, 500 yards north in rolling tundra.

The disturbed bruin had captured her meal at the edge of the foothills, an area more risky for caribou because of the abundance of bears.

"During the calving and post-calving periods we find a majority of our bears in the foothills," Young said. He believes bears prefer the foothills because they offer greater habitat diversity than the coastal plain. Opportunistic foragers, bears find a variety of berries and other plants among the different elevations and soil types of the foothills. They find a greater abundance of ground squirrels in the hills and better denning sites. The rugged topography also provides escape terrain for sows, who, except for the breeding season, avoid male bears.

The relatively low number of bears on the coastal plain, Young said, is hypothesized as one reason caribou have historically calved there. His work suggests that caribou calf survival may decline if the herd is displaced from the coastal plain to the foothills as a consequence of oil development.

THE BIOLOGIST'S ROLE

Field work — watching and handling animals, flying, camping out — was in Young's mind's eye when he first enrolled in the University of Idaho's wildlife biology program in 1976. Today, after 10 years as a biologist, the lure of field work remains, but the opportunity seems to be shrinking.

"For every hour I spend in the field on this project," Young said, "I'm in front of a computer screen about 10."

After entering the data from the two-month field season, he runs nine or 10 programs for analysis and interpretation. The result: The movements and habitat use of individual bears and bear populations are quantified, and related to both the distribution of caribou and calf mortality.

While few involved in the development verses preservation issue doubt the importance of biological information for decision making and management purposes, the Inupiat community of Kaktovik that serves as the base for most of the biological research and some recreationists express reservations about radio-telemetry work.

They charge that the collars bother the animals and the capture process is too disturbing.

Young empathizes with the different perspective and concedes that his bears are stressed during capture. But, except for the capturing, he doesn't think the bears mind participating in his study.

His relocation flights only disturb each animal for a few minutes, once or twice a week during the calving and post-calving season. "And the lightweight collars we use today (about two pounds) are less than 2 percent of the average bear's body weight," he says. "Our observations indicate no change in the animals behavior or activity. After a while I think they're virtually unnoticed by the bear."

Young feels the temporary stress his research causes to some individual animals is small in comparison to the value of the information to the population as a whole. Unlike some segments of the public, biologists must focus on the welfare of populations, rather than individuals.

"Management of populations is where the future of the species lies," he said, adding that in a larger sense, his work helps to maintain natural functioning of the entire Arctic Refuge ecosystem.

What bear 1516 unwittingly reveals about its interactions with caribou and other species, as well as its habitat requirements, can be

BELOW LEFT: Gerald Garner inspects the inside of a bear den in the foothills of the Brooks Range in the Arctic National Wildlife Refuge. Pregnant female grizzlies in northern Alaska may spend up to eight months in their dens. (Larry Martin, USFWS)

BELOW: Another of Alaska's contingent of experienced bear researchers is Vic Barnes, shown here measuring a solution to anesthetize bears in the Kodiak National Wildlife Refuge. (Marion Stirrup)

Tom McCabe and Tom Servelo weigh a grizzly caught within the Arctic National Wildlife Refuge. Female grizzlies on the North Slope average about 220 pounds. Bears may gain a hundred pounds during the summer feeding season to replenish their body fat for winter hibernation. (Don Young, USFWS)

used to predict and minimize the ecological cost of proposed habitat modification, Young says. The information can be used to designate key habitat areas or to restrict industrial activities during critical periods. It can help locate roads, pipelines and facilities to lessen their effect on wildlife. It can also improve management of sport and subsistence hunting of bears.

Research-based information, specific and quantifiable, becomes increasingly vital, Young says, as we seek to minimize disruption of wildlife and their habitats in the face of man's expanding encroachment.

**Meet the
Bagoys of Alaska
...see page 104**

ALASKA'S REINDEER

By Bill Sherwonit

Editor's note: *Introduction of animals to various parts of Alaska has been the source of controversy for decades. For an overview of various introduced species in the state, please see "Alaska's Alien Animals" by Edgar P. Bailey in Vol. 19, No. 3, Kodiak.*

Until winter 1992, few Alaskans had heard of, let alone visited, Hagemeister Island. But by late November, Hagemeister was a household name throughout much of the state, and had gained considerable notoriety outside Alaska, as well.

A 23-mile-long island in Bristol Bay, about 19 miles from the Yup'ik village of Togiak, Hagemeister is the site of a reindeer-herding project that, left unmanaged, spiraled out of control with tragic consequences.

Last November, forced to deal with a herd that had depleted its winter range and thus faced massive starvation, the federal government conducted a well-intentioned reindeer mercy killing. But by mid-December, that kill-off — viewed by critics as a senseless slaughter and waste of meat — had become a

holiday-season public-relations disaster for the government.

In the end, U.S. Fish and Wildlife Service shooters killed 742 of Hagemeister's reindeer. Meat from 172 of those animals was distributed to Alaska Natives residing in the region but the remainder was left to rot, after the aircraft used to haul carcasses was damaged during a landing on Hagemeister. Another 122 reindeer were removed from the island in a highly publicized

Reindeer on Hagemeister Island in Bristol Bay became the focus of much attention in fall 1992 when officials of U.S. Fish and Wildlife Service shot many of the animals because the herd had outgrown the island's carrying capacity. (Tom Soucek)

airlift rescue spearheaded by a Nome-area doctor named Don Olson. And 193 were left alive on the island, to survive the winter as best they could.

At the center of last winter's controversy was the Fish and Wildlife Service, which has been responsible for the island since Hagemeister was added to the Alaska Maritime National Wildlife Refuge in 1980. But the holiday slaughter was simply one step in a reindeer herding scheme that perhaps was doomed from the start, especially when viewed in the larger context of Alaska's reindeer industry.

Reindeer herding was begun on Hagemeister during the mid-1960s, when the Bureau of Indian Affairs (BIA), responsible for overseeing the industry since 1937, loaned 144 reindeer to three Yup'ik residents of Togiak as seeds for an island herd.

The BIA; Bureau of Land Management, which then owned the land; and University of Alaska were expected to conduct studies and provide technical assistance to the herders, as part of a plan to stimulate economic development within the region. Reindeer experts initially figured the island's carrying capacity to be 1,000 to 3,000 animals.

Grazing management was minimal to non-existent, however, and by 1973 there was evidence of deteriorating range. A reduction to 450 animals was recommended, and accomplished, that year, but

within two years, the herd exceeded 800 reindeer. Despite the evidence of problems, reindeer grazing on Hagemeister was allowed by special permit even after the refuge was created in 1980.

Refuge managers met with the reindeer's owner — by this time, only Jacob Gosuk remained from the original three permittees — several times during the 1980s. But little changed. With virtually no active management and no natural predators to keep numbers down, the herd continued to grow. In 1990, a peak of 1,530 animals was counted.

Several hundred reindeer died during each of the next two winters, convincing the government it could wait no longer. The Fish and Wildlife

Service acquired the Hagemeister herd in June 1992, for the bargain price of $1, then tried to give it away through BIA's Reindeer Loan Program. When that attempt met with only limited success, the agency mounted its mercy kill mission.

State and federal reindeer experts really shouldn't have been surprised by what happened on Hagemeister. Island reindeer herding has historically proved disastrous. As Dave Swanson and Daniel LaPlant of the Soil Conservation Service reported in 1987, "Reindeer on Hagemeister Island have been subjected to a typical island-management syndrome that has been repeated many times: reindeer are introduced to a pristine environment that has abundant lichen resources and

the herd increases at a rate of 30 percent per year. Effective grazing management is not used and the lichen resources then become depleted and a decline in the reindeer population follows, usually a result of winter starvation."

The classic reindeer island-management syndrome occurred on St. Matthew Island in the Bering Sea, where 29 reindeer were introduced in 1944. By 1963, the herd numbered 6,000 animals. And the following winter, nearly all died. Only 42 reindeer remained in 1966. And they too eventually disappeared, according to a 1992 report in *Rangifer*, the Scientific Journal of Reindeer and Reindeer Husbandry.

Similar boom-and-bust cycles — which Swanson calls "eruptive oscillations" — have been reported on Nunivak, St. Lawrence and St. Paul islands. In each instance, unmanaged reindeer herds increased dramatically, only to suffer population crashes from starvation.

Though not as disastrous as what happened on Hagemeister or St. Matthew islands, Alaska's reindeer industry as a whole has experienced dramatic fluctuations since its birth in the 1890s.

Villagers from Wales strive to control a reindeer trying to escape from a chute during the annual clipping of antlers at Wales on the Seward Peninsula. (Penny Rennick)

ABOVE: *Reindeer roam the coastal hills just inland from Cape Woolley in early June. (Penny Rennick)*

LEFT: *There are 21 families and 16 communities represented in the Reindeer Herders Association in Alaska. Larry Davis oversees one of herds closest to Nome. (Charles Mason)*

The industry's origins can be traced to Sheldon Jackson, the government's general agent for education, who imported reindeer from Siberia to aid Alaska Natives living in the state's northwest region.

But before exploring Jackson's role and the industry's evolution, it seems appropriate to briefly discuss reindeer biology.

Reindeer are the domestic relatives of caribou. There are, the experts say, few differences in behavior or appearance to distinguish reindeer from caribou, which both belong to the species *Rangifer tarandus* and can successfully interbreed. Reindeer, as a rule, tend to be smaller in size and lighter or more spotted in color than their wild cousins. They reach sexual maturity in their second year and may live 10 to 15 years.

Being social animals, reindeer, like caribou, gather in herds that move with the seasons, although their migrations occur on a much smaller scale.

Calving, which occurs at roughly the same site year after year, begins in mid-April and continues through May. Most cows have a single calf. After birth, and as summer approaches, newborn calves and their mothers tend to separate briefly from the herd; apparently it's during this time that calves learn to recognize their mothers.

In summer, reindeer migrate to high, windy places, such as ridge tops, or to breezy lake and ocean shorelines, to escape the persecution of warble flies, blackflies, mosquitoes and other flying insects. The adults of both sexes begin regrowing their antlers, which become fully developed by July. The antlers are covered by a soft, furlike material that resembles velvet. The velvet is rubbed off by late summer or fall, leaving males with hardened antlers for the rut, which begins in September and lasts into October. Autumn also is marked by movement inland as reindeer seek more protected areas.

In winter, herds head for open forest or wind-swept slopes where they have easy access to lichens, their main food source until spring. The relationship between reindeer and their winter range is critical. Lichens grow extremely slowly; when overgrazed or burned, they may take several decades to regenerate.

In some areas of the world, Scandinavia and Siberia, for example, reindeer have been bred as domesticated animals for centuries. But Alaska has been in the reindeer business for only a little more than 100 years. It all began with Sheldon Jackson's desire to help Northwest Alaska's Natives. Help that was not necessarily needed, according to Dorothy Jean Ray, author of *The Eskimos of Bering Strait, 1650-1898* (1983).

Following his first-ever trip to the Arctic in 1890, Jackson concluded that "the Eskimo race was dying out," Ray reported. "Jackson's judgment was made without knowledge of the real character of Eskimo life....In 1890, Eskimos were in no greater danger of extinction than generations before."

Despite considerable opposition, Jackson used private funds to transport 16 reindeer from Siberia to Unalaska and Amaknak islands in the Aleutians in September 1891. All died from lack of sufficient forage, but that failed to deter Jackson, who arranged for the shipment of another 1,280 reindeer to the Seward Peninsula between 1892 and 1902. Initially, Siberian herders instructed local Natives in reindeer-herding techniques. But they were replaced by Lapp herders from Scandinavia in 1894.

By 1902, Alaska's herds included more than 5,000 reindeer. But few were owned by Natives. Jackson instead gave reindeer to mission churches for eventual distribution to Eskimos, as well as to Lapps hired as teachers. Even as early as the mid-1890s, Ray noted, "Jackson held no steadfast course toward the goal as originally conceived, that is, for the exclusive interests of the Eskimo people....Jackson was thinking not of food for the Eskimos, but of food for the vast non-Eskimo world...."

Such thinking got Jackson removed from office in 1906 and a new policy was instituted, emphasizing Native ownership. By 1916, more than 1,200 Eskimos owned reindeer, but their average herd size was less than 50 animals, not nearly enough to reap economic benefits. The Lapps and mission churches continued to profit most from the fledgling industry.

From the midteens until the early 1930s, Alaska's reindeer industry experienced tremendous growth — and still more controversy. In 1914, about 58,000 reindeer roamed the state; by 1932, that number had jumped to an all-time high of 641,000. Reindeer herding had become a big business, for at least a few aggressive non-Native entrepreneurs.

Chief players in this new era were the Lomen brothers, Carl, Alfred and Ralph, who bought into the reindeer business through Lomen and Co., the family's Nome-based operation. Between 1914 and 1929, they purchased some 14,000 animals. Their plan was to establish a market for reindeer meat in the Lower 48. And they had at least some degree of success: From 1928 to 1930, for example, more than 5 million pounds of reindeer meat was reportedly shipped outside the territory.

Although their marketing energies were primarily focused outside Alaska, the Lomens' aggressive entry into the reindeer industry created tensions with Native herders. And, at least in some instances, their successes were at the expense of Eskimos. Too, cattlemen from western states in the Lower 48 complained about competition from reindeer meat. Inevitably, questions were raised about the appropriateness, and legality, of such a non-Native enterprise.

By the early 1930s, the Lomens had earned a reputation among some as "unlawful interlopers" who'd unfairly taken reindeer ranges from Native herders and used unethical, if not illegal, practices in building their business.

Concerns about the Lomens' growing economic influence finally prompted the government to investigate Alaska's reindeer industry. And on Sept. 1, 1937, Congress passed the Alaska Reindeer Act, which prohibited non-Native ownership of reindeer.

The 1930s marked another dramatic change in the reindeer industry: the start of a population crash. By 1940 reindeer numbers had fallen to about 253,000, less than half the 1932 peak. The population bottomed out a decade later, when only 25,000 reindeer were counted statewide.

The dramatic decline was attributed to several interrelated factors: wolf predation; winter-range destruction by overgrazing, trampling and fire; poor herd and range management; disease; changing caribou migration routes that resulted in many reindeer joining caribou herds; herder conflicts; poor facilities and low-profit margins.

The industry began a gradual resurgence in the 1950s, but numbers have never again approached those of 1932, or even exceeded 50,000 animals.

Today, Alaska's reindeer population numbers between 35,000 and 43,000 animals. Of that total, some 23,000 to 28,000 are distributed among 14 permit holders on the Seward Peninsula,

The heads and antlers of some of Hagemeister Island's reindeer provide a grisly sight. Of the 742 animals killed on Hagemeister in 1992, the meat from 172 was salvaged and distributed to Natives living in the region. (Tom Soucek)

which Dave Swanson of the Soil Conservation Service says is "very suited to reindeer herding. It has suitable vegetation and the necessary diversity of ecosystems and topography. The ocean front is a great advantage in summer, when reindeer need to escape heat and insects."

Another significant reindeer operation, with 6,000 to 8,000

For the past 20 years or so, reindeer antlers sold for the oriental market have been the most profitable sector of the reindeer industry. Korea has traditionally been the biggest purchaser of antlers from Alaska, but in December 1992 the Korean government ruled that reindeer antlers could not be sold as natural medicine because reindeer antlers are not listed in their official folk medicine guides. (Charles Mason)

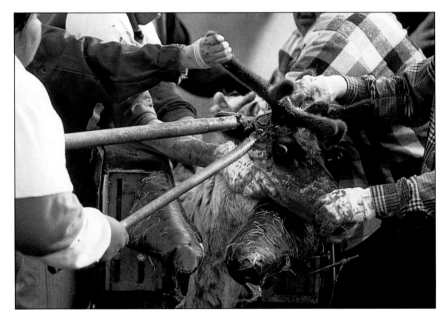

animals, is based on Nunivak Island. Smaller herds are also located on Umnak, Kodiak, Atka, St. Lawrence, St. Paul, St. George and Stuart islands and a couple of reindeer farms have been established on the Kenai Peninsula. The state also manages a herd at Point MacKenzie near Anchorage.

Most herds are owned by individuals or families, although Native corporations have had limited involvement. The BIA itself owns about 1,800 reindeer, available for loan to new herders. The owners then have seven years to pay back BIA the same number of animals they were initially loaned.

In recent years, at least one non-Native Alaskan has also owned a small commercial reindeer herd, but a government panel has ruled that operation to be unlawful.

Tom Williams of Palmer began building his herd of more than 200 reindeer in the late 1980s, by purchasing reindeer in Canada and transporting them to his Matanuska Valley farm. For several years he sold meat to local markets, as well as live reindeer to Lower 48 ranchers. He also allowed tourists to pet and feed his animals — for a fee.

In November 1992, following a lawsuit by the Nome-based Reindeer Herders' Association, the federal government's Board of Indian Appeals ruled that only Natives can run commercial reindeer operations in Alaska, even if the animals were brought into the state, which Williams saw as a loophole to the 1937 Reindeer Act. The board also recommended that the BIA either buy, or condemn, Williams' herd. In early December 1992, the BIA's Alaska regional office gave Williams six months to dispose of his herd.

Don Tomlin, BIA's reindeer specialist, says that, given the reindeer's importation from Canada, he was content to "let Williams do his thing," as long as the Palmer operation remained small. But Tomlin adds that there's good reason for the Natives-only restriction: "If anyone could get into it, within two or three years most Natives would be out of business, they'd be offered so much money. And you have to remember the industry was started to benefit the Native population."

Traditionally, Alaska's Native herders have blended their reindeer operations with other subsistence activities. "The way they've managed their herds has fit in real well with the subsistence lifestyle," Tomlin says.

Reindeer are carefully monitored during the spring calving season and a June handling, during which antlers are harvested and calves and steers are marked. But they are then allowed to "fend for themselves" through the rest of the summer. Slaughtering is done in early winter, after the first heavy freeze and snowfall, when reindeer are in their best condition and snow machines dramatically increase human mobility. Most slaughtering takes place out on the range, without corralling. There they are shot, skinned, gutted and washed. "Usually there's one shooter and a half-dozen or so skinners," Tomlin says. "The shooter drops as many animals as he can before the herd gets spooked."

A second handling is done in midwinter, usually January, during which the reindeer are given shots to combat warble-fly infestations and brucellosis, a form of venereal disease specific to reindeer and caribou.

Overall, Tomlin says, reindeer herding is "a very inexact science. But that's the way it has to be, if it's going to be part of a subsistence lifestyle."

There are some, however, who would like to see a bigger and better managed industry. Lyle Renecker, for instance. Renecker, with the University of Alaska Fairbanks' Reindeer Research Program, sees the potential for an expanded reindeer industry, one that relies more heavily on meat sales to the Lower 48 and less on antler sales to Asia.

Sales of antlers covered in velvet became an important part of Alaska's reindeer industry about two decades ago. Today, Renecker says, they are its primary driving force. This remains true despite a dramatic drop in prices during the past year, caused by black-market sales of Russian antler to Korea, the world's largest buyer. Korea subsequently halted all imports of reindeer antler, causing a price crash. But, he adds, "antler sales are driving the industry in the wrong direction. The emphasis must be on meat production if the industry is going to grow."

Renecker would like to see reindeer meat more aggressively marketed as a specialty item that appeals to a more health-conscious America. "Reindeer meat is more nutritious than beef," he says. "It's lower in cholesterol and fat and higher in protein. There's a lot of room for expansion of the reindeer industry, if it's more closely regulated and properly marketed. But we need to produce a product that's appealing, one that has more consistent quality."

The state of Alaska strongly supports expansion of the reindeer industry, says Doug Witte with the Alaska Department of Natural Resources. "The one big thing the industry needs is a consistent supply of high quality red meat. Most reindeer now are intensively managed only twice a year and then left to run free. We need operations that provide red meat 12 months a year. There are ways of doing that other than just frozen red meat. It's possible to have canned products, stew, sausage or grocery store items."

To meet its goals, the state would like to have more intensive farming, rather than herding. And it's also concerned about equal access to reindeer operations and appropriate grazing-lease fees.

As it enters its second century, Alaska's reindeer industry faces numerous challenges if it is to expand and prosper. Perhaps the biggest step will be to learn from past mistakes. Like the island management syndrome, for example. Which brings us back where we began: Hagemeister Island.

In mid-March 1993, the Fish and Wildlife Service counted 184 reindeer, survivors of the government's kill-off and the winter season. According to a cooperative reindeer management plan agreed to by the Fish and Wildlife Service, BIA and Togiak Traditional Council, Hagemeister's remaining reindeer were to be

Reindeer make a run for it during a herding operation at White Mountain. (Charles Mason)

allowed to stay on the island through August 1993. In September, the three parties, working together, would remove all healthy reindeer and airlift them to the mainland.

In late August, U.S. Fish and Wildlife Service officials herded the remaining reindeer on Hagemeister, estimated to be just under 300, into special corrals where the animals were inoculated. From there they were flown to Point MacKenzie near Anchorage to a farm managed by the state with inmates from a state correctional facility as workers. Any animals not suitable for relocation were to be slaughtered on the island, with their meat to be distributed to Togiak residents.

As for the 120 animals that Don Olson rescued from

Hagemeister last November? Forty-one died during the winter, Tomlin reported, at least partly because of mismanagement of the reindeer after they'd been taken to Goose Bay, across Cook Inlet from Anchorage. About two-thirds of the survivors were to be sold live to a rancher in Texas and the remainder were to be put on public display, at least for the summer, with elk and bison at a tourist attraction near Portage.

It seems a suitably peculiar ending to one of the stranger, and more tragic, chapters in the history of Alaska's reindeer industry.

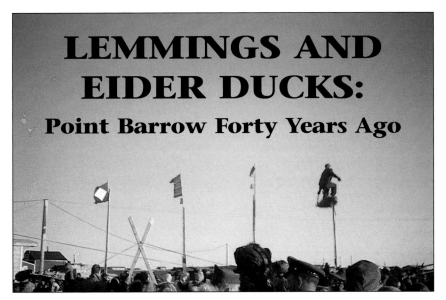

LEMMINGS AND EIDER DUCKS:
Point Barrow Forty Years Ago

By Dick Person

Editor's note: *An experienced writer and outdoorsman, Dick lives near Teslin Lake in Yukon Territory.*

A shimmering wave of 500 eiders appears on the horizon over Eielson Lagoon, just east of the ages-old duck hunting camp of the Eskimos. Counting them by checking the number in the field of view of my 7-by-50 binoculars, I quickly scan the approaching line of ducks, mentally calculating the total number based on multiples of that first view-field.

The first overhead pass is quite high, but the ducks circle in a figure-eight pattern and pass over again — this time hardly 100 feet above me. Behind my parked Weasel (a U.S. Army World War II all-terrain vehicle), staccato shots break out and, as I turn, I see birds falling to the ground. How many? Pacific (common) or king eider? I'll check with the hunters later, but now I need to stay with the birds while they are on the move. It is important to get an accurate estimate of the eider migration as a whole, as well as the number taken by the Native hunters.

Such are the elements of thesis material for a master of arts in wildlife management.

As a teen-ager, I'd been introduced to Robert Service's poems of the far North and developed a longing to see and to live in Alaska and the Yukon. Growing up on the north shore of Lake Superior was ideal for one who loved wild places. The skills necessary for bush living were developed there. After a stint in the U.S. Army Airborne in the Far East, I returned to pursue natural history studies at the University of Minnesota, Duluth. Upon graduation in 1952, I was looking for a well-paid job because I had the possibility of graduate school in mind.

Some friends returning that spring from Alaska mentioned high wages in the Anchorage area. Borrowing money for plane

fare, a friend and I eagerly set forth. We spent the summer working for the Alaska Railroad laying new wide-gauge track from Portage to Whittier. Each day we'd lay track for six hours, then spike it for another six hours. We really learned what John Henry's "steel driving" was all about.

After a winter in graduate studies at the University of Missouri, I was invited to do field work at Point Barrow with funding by the Arctic Institute of North America and the Office of Naval Research.

Spring 1953 found me flying to the Arctic on a "Flying Boxcar" (C82 or C119 cargo planes that were used for dropping parachuters). Impressions of that flight still linger: Denali, like a queen with the lesser peaks of her court gathered around,

Displaying the skill of an experienced blanket toss participant, this contestant twirls an inflated sea mammal bladder while being tossed aloft from the walrus-hide blanket during a 1953 celebration. (Dick Person)

all wearing ermine; north of Fairbanks the number of meandering rivers and oxbow lakes, the Yukon, the forks of the Koyukuk, the John, and then Anaktuvuk Pass. Quickly the Brooks Range fell behind, and the vastness of the arctic coastal plain spread before us. The literally countless number of tundra ponds and lakes we could only comprehend with the same wonder we feel about outer space and astronomical distances. Still frozen, these ponds were readily discernible against the brown tundra of early June.

Beyond the tundra, lay the hemi-circle of the ice pack of the Chukchi and Beaufort seas, which meet here on an imaginary line drawn northward from Point Barrow.

On the ground at Barrow, we were struck by the finely sorted gravel of the broad beaches and bare areas that lacked plant cover. The ubiquitous nature of this fine gravel is due mainly to existing and pre-existing mountain ranges to the south that have contributed detritus to the coastal plain.

Within hours of arriving, I was introduced to the personnel of the Naval Arctic Research Lab and fell into a mixed routine of lab work and daily forays into the field to make wildlife observations and collect hard data.

I was field assistant to Dan Thompson, an instructor from the University of Missouri, who had provided the opportunity to go to Barrow. Dan was completing his fourth season of study on lemmings, whose population was expected to peak this summer, the fourth year in this species' four-year population cycle.

My own research would involve documenting the eider duck migration: its magnitude, periodicity, sex and species composition, the extent of Native hunting and its impact on eider numbers. I began a daily two-hour watch in the evenings (the period of greatest flight activity) and extended that later to a two-hour shift every four hours around the clock.

Anyone who chooses to study the life of almost any plant or animal in a particular environment will soon learn that virtually every other living, and non-living, element is involved to a greater or lesser extent. For example, the grasses and sedges of the tundra, before the summer's growth began, looked as though God had shears and

had decided to clip every blade to ground level. This, of course, was the impact of a burgeoning lemming population under the snow cover. As new growth occurred, Dan Thompson; John Koranda, another field assistant; and I measured its progress and watched as it was eagerly consumed by these rodents. The lemmings ate only the lower one-third of the new shoots, which when measured for food value were found to have 90 percent of the nutrients. The remainder of the shoots dried and formed windrows under which the lemmings lived and moved to avoid avian predation.

Although snowy owls had congregated in the area in large numbers, drawn by the peak lemming population, the principal overhead predators were jaegers, which nested and raised their young in well-defined territories on the tundra. Most numerous were pomarine jaegers, though parasitic and long-tailed varieties were also present.

The timing of phenologic events was fascinating: The

TOP RIGHT: *Bill Maher studies a jaeger chick, which studies him in turn at the Naval Arctic Research Lab. (Dick Person)*

RIGHT: *Inupiat of Barrow still hunt waterfowl at the lagoons near Barrow. Here the late Harry Brower Sr. and his son, Eugene, display of pair of eiders collected during a fall hunt some years ago. (Penny Rennick)*

LEFT: *Field researchers have many talents. This group has formed the first Barrow Quartet, consisting of Ed Clebsch on flute, Sim Drew on harmonica, Dr. Shanks on tonette and John Koranda on tenor recorder. (Dick Person)*

BOTTOM RIGHT: *Fellow field assistant John Koranda cuts Dick Person's hair during a break in the research on lemmings and waterfowl at Barrow. (Courtesy of Dick Person)*

BOTTOM LEFT: *From left, Quentin Tomich, Bill Thompson and Paul Hurd hold this string of whitefish on the steps of the ichthyology lab at the former U.S. Naval Arctic Research Laboratory. The facility has subsequently been turned over to the Barrow village corporation that operates a hotel, restaurant, offices and laboratories here. (Dick Person)*

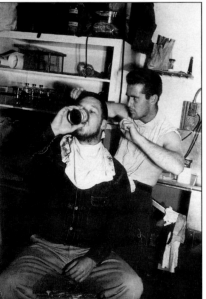

first batch of young lemmings appeared with the initial vigorous growth of forage plants just as the jaeger hatchlings needed lemming young to begin and augment their growth. The summer research proceeded: We followed the growth, physiology and behavior of the lemmings, the plants and the predators, including the least weasel, the arctic fox and the snowy owl. When the lemming population finally peaked, many of the animals were in a nutritional tailspin and exhibited bizarre behavior such as showing aggression to humans in their vicinity.

As the number of lemming-to-lemming encounters in their burrows increased, which we monitored with electrical sensors, a state of mass hysteria was reached that resulted in the lemmings' emigration from the tundra to the arctic ice. During that period I came upon snowy owls so stuffed with lemmings that they could not get off the ground to fly away.

My own studies with the eiders resulted in base-line data that could be used for comparison with future abundance. Harvest figures from the Natives indicated the Inupiat hunters were taking less than 1 percent of the migratory birds.

The spring whale hunt celebration, known as *nalukataq*, was the highlight of the season in Barrow. Ritual dances by the hunters and their mates portrayed the drama of the taking of the bowhead whales, and the integral connection of these people with the sea. Skin-drum rhythms reaching back to the time of Beringia accompanied these enacted tales of hardship, patient waiting and adventure.

The most spectacular activity of the celebrants was the blanket toss. For this, walrus hides were sewn into a large square and hand loops were attached to the square all along its edge. Around the sides of the square people aligned themselves, grasping the loop with the right hand. In unison they lifted on the hide and the dancer standing in the middle of the square was catapulted to ever-increasing heights while moving to maintain balance and display skill. At times a dancer would reach elevations four to five times greater than her individual height. Women commonly participated in this strenuous activity and were some of the most proficient performers. The most skilled whirled an inflated sea mammal bladder around themselves like a jump rope, while aloft.

I expressed a desire to try this sport, and they made way for me. My height increased with each succeeding toss, and on the third one, as I looked down, the hide appeared like a postage stamp below me. My curiosity had been more than satisfied, much to the amusement of the onlookers who must have seen the expressions on my face.

Muktuk (whale skin and blubber) fuels these high-energy pastimes, and the blanket toss was my introduction to this prized traditional food. I was offered a slice from the fluke and found its flavor like a blend between cashews and fish. However, its apparent softness in the mouth was deceptive. The more I chewed the more it grew, and I finally swallowed it whole, with a big gulp of coffee.

Our food, that summer at the research lab, was remarkable for its quality and abundance. A small crew of roughnecks was doing experimental oil and gas drilling nearby, so we were able to eat with them in a common mess hall. A chef from a large

hotel in New York City was in charge, and the variety and excellence of our meals would have done credit to a fine restaurant. Saturday night, especially, would feature steaks, seafoods and gala desserts. Such cuisine, I was told, was part of a plan to maintain high morale among oil workers in remote places. For me, as a graduate student on a tight budget, the fine fare was an unexpected bonus.

Also on Saturday night all the lab personnel would gather to hear about other research. For some, the lab was mainly a staging area for expeditions onto the ice pack to do marine biology or for trips to raft the northward-flowing rivers of the Brooks Range to study anthropological sites. Other reports dealt with geology of ice wedging, population dynamics of everything from insects to beluga whales, archaeology of a nearby pre-Barrow site, glacial

and current climatology and many other subjects.

In addition to my overall impressions of the Arctic, the people of Barrow and its environs, I was deeply struck by

the narrow zone between sky and tundra in which life exists here, and its high degree of fragility. The word "ecology" had assumed new worlds of meaning for me.

TOP RIGHT: The subject of Dick Person's research at Barrow 40 years ago was eider ducks, such as king eiders like this pair photographed on the North Slope many years later. (John W. Warden)

RIGHT: The lowlands near Barrow are dotted with numerous ponds, perfect habitat for waterfowl, shorebirds, and in some years an abundance of rodents and other small mammals. This photo shows the town of Barrow taken from the road heading northeast toward Point Barrow, northernmost land in the United States. (Randy Brandon)

The Bagoys of Alaska

By Richard P. Emanuel

Through the battle, through defeat,
moving yet and never stopping,
Pioneers! O Pioneers!
　　　　　　　—Walt Whitman

Like many Alaska pioneers, John Bagoy was lured north by the glint of gold. From the Klondike gold rush through stampedes to Nome, Fairbanks and Iditarod, to entrepeneurial ventures in Flat and early Anchorage, Bagoy and his family cut a wide swath through the last century of Alaska history. Yet like most gold-seekers, their legacy does not lie in mineral wealth. The Bagoys made their mark on Alaska through persistence of spirit, wit and work.

Bagoy was born John Benedict Fabian Bajoye in the Croatian province of Dalmatia, in 1869. Then as now, Bagoy's homeland was a land of strife. His parents were peasant farmers who raised olives and grapes in the mountainous countryside. Dalmatia was part of the Austrian empire and when he came of age, young Bagoy served a three-year stint in Emperor Franz Joseph's army. Six months after his release from service, he was recalled. Disenchanted with the Austrian army, Bagoy fled to America. He landed on Ellis Island, New York, in 1894.

Bagoy's youngest son, John, 71, of Anchorage, takes up his father's story. "He couldn't speak English when he got here," John says.

Through a Dalmatian countryman, he found work digging sewer ditches, a job he held long enough to pick up some cash and some English. Then he lit out for the California gold fields. Somewhere along the way he Americanized his name, changing the spelling from Bajoye to Bagoy.

In a Sierra Nevada gold mine, Bagoy learned the dangerous craft of blasting. Better pay lured him north to the Treadwell Mine on Douglas Island, near Juneau. He was already in Alaska in 1898 when news of a fabulous gold strike touched off a rush to Canada's Klondike River. Bagoy joined the stampede.

"He got to Skagway all right but he didn't have enough money to go over the pass," John says. Canadian "Mounties" in Chilkoot Pass required a year's provisions — a grubstake of roughly 1,000 pounds — before they would let a prospector enter Yukon Territory. Undaunted, Bagoy staggered up the Chilkoot Trail at first beneath other miners' goods. "He would pack loads up at $1 a pound," John says, "and that's how he earned his grubstake."

When Bagoy reached Dawson City there was still gold to be had. "He had a partner and they staked a piece of ground on Yonker Creek, up around Bonanza," says John.

FAR LEFT: *The ultimate pioneer, John Bagoy, born in 1869, gathered his Croatian energy and work ethic and followed his dreams of riches to the Klondike, to Nome, Fairbanks, Iditarod and finally Anchorage. He made it to the Klondike when there was still good ground to be staked, fared poorly at Nome, and lost his savings in the collapse of a California bank while he was searching for a bride in his homeland. (Courtesy of the Bagoy family)*

LEFT: *Using promises of wealth and adventure, John Bagoy convinced Marie Antoinette Vlahucic of Bosnia-Herzegovina to be his bride. The couple arrived in the United States in 1907; by 1908 they were on their way to Alaska. (Courtesy of the Bagoy family)*

"And they did pretty good." In two years of digging and sluicing, the partners laid up a sizeable poke. Then came word in 1900 that the beaches of Nome bore gold. Bagoy sold his Klondike claim and rushed down the Yukon River toward Nome. But his luck failed and after a disappointing adventure he sailed to California.

For a time, Bagoy ran a wine and grocery story out of a tent near Bakersfield, Calif. With a brother, he also sought silver and gold in Nevada. In 1906, Bagoy became a U.S. citizen. He left his store with his brother, deposited $10,000 in a San Francisco bank and returned to Europe to look for a wife.

In a village in Bosnia-Herzegovina, Bagoy found Marie Antoinette Vlahucic. She was barely 20. Bagoy, 37, impressed her with tales of the faraway Yukon — and with his bankroll. They married, honeymooned in France and sailed to America, arriving in June 1907. If Marie expected a life of romance and ease, at least she got romance.

Ease was a different matter. The bank where Bagoy had placed his money had collapsed, taking his fortune with it. With his last cash, he took his bride to Nevada and there he toiled in a silver mine. They lived in a tent on the desert where burros ate clothes off the clothesline, according to family legend. Their first child, Peter, was born in early 1908. The burros loved his diapers.

Bagoy soon heard stories of gold being mined near Fairbanks. "He had gold fever," John says, "I mean there's no two ways about it." When Peter was two months old, the family headed to San Francisco by stagecoach, then north to Alaska by steamship, train and riverboat. Bagoy staked a claim on a creek outside Fairbanks. He dug a shaft while his bride cranked a windlass and hauled up dirt which she piled for later sluicing.

"They spent their first winter out there in misery," John says. They lived in a floorless tent in darkness and temperatures reaching -50 degrees F. Heat from the wood stove turned the permafrost to mud. Marie piled more spruce bows each day on their beds as they sank into the thawing earth from the heat of their bodies.

In midwinter, Bagoy decided the ground he had staked was no good so the family moved to another claim. That failed too and the family moved into town. While her husband worked at odd jobs, Marie took in laundry. They were expecting their second child. The baby boy was in breach position and died during birth, in September 1909.

Word of a gold strike in Iditarod reached Fairbanks in early 1910. With nothing to lose, the Bagoys made the two-week river journey to Alaska's latest mosquito-infested boomtown. This time, rather than seek the elusive gold in the ground, Bagoy sought the gold in prospectors' pockets. He formed a partnership to deliver water around town. He tended bar, unloaded barges and worked at other jobs. He built an 18- by 20-foot log cabin chinked with moss and boasting a rough plank floor. There, Marie bore Doris, her first daughter and the first white child born in Iditarod, in November 1910.

By 1913, most Iditarod miners had moved to Flat, seven miles up Otter Creek from Iditarod. Flat and Discovery, three more miles up the creek, sprang up near the richest

By 1917 John and Marie Bagoy were beginning to cultivate the plants that would eventually make their floral shops so well-known in southcentral Alaska. Here the family makes their way among produce raised for the miners at Flat. From left are Mary, Eileen, Marie, Doris, Pete and John Bagoy. (Courtesy of the Bagoy family)

gold-bearing ground. Bagoy bought a roadhouse in Discovery. It had 12 bunks plus a bar with billiards, pool and card tables. Bagoy managed the roadhouse and tended bar while his wife cooked meals and baked bread and desserts for 20 to 40 men a day. In November 1913, she bore a second daughter, Mary, the couple's third surviving child.

Bagoy was forced to move in early 1914. One of the biggest landholders in the district claimed the land where the roadhouse stood and said he planned to mine it. Bagoy bought another roadhouse but a year later the same thing happened. Bagoy refused to budge a second time so the miner's dredge sliced into the roadhouse. Card tables, bunks, barrels of whiskey — all were washed into the dredge pond. A sympathetic friend invited

Bagoy to take over yet another roadhouse, this time in Flat itself. The friend later struck it rich and gave him the place. It was called "John Bagoy's Three-Time-Move Saloon." The third Bagoy daughter, Eileen, was born there, in August 1915.

Mining in the Iditarod district was in decline in 1917. The U.S. entered World War I in April and able-bodied young men were soon scarce. That summer, the Bagoys sold their roadhouse and bought a six-acre farm on Otter Creek. It came with a large greenhouse, a root cellar and a two-bedroom house. The soil was good, the summer was hot and the family began to grow vegetables for local sale. "Of course, that's what he should have done all along," says John. "Basically, he was a farmer."

After less than a year on the farm, the spring of 1918 brought ice-jams and a flood. The greenhouse and root cellar were washed out but Marie would not leave her flooding house. She was pulled out in time but the house filled with mud 2 feet deep. Unbowed, Bagoy and his friends shoveled out the mud, raised the house on skids and dragged it to higher ground. He built a new greenhouse, expanded the house, cleared more land and planted anew. What grew this time was fleeting prosperity, a few seasons of success.

The Bagoys supplied the only fresh produce for sale in Flat and Iditarod: tomatoes, cucumbers, lettuce, potatoes. They acquired chickens and a cow and sold milk. Young Peter began to cut firewood, take the cow to pasture and deliver milk to customers. In the winter, he fetched water by rolling a frozen barrel into the kitchen. Also in winter, Lapp reindeer herders drove their herd onto the Bagoy farm for butchering. In return, Bagoy got his pick of the herd. In 1919, Marie bore a fourth daughter, Gabrielle.

Flat and Iditarod were shrinking when the older Bagoy children reached school age. In 1911, the two settlements had totaled more than 1,000 people; nine years later, barely 200 remained. The Bagoys decided to leave but they needed money to make the move. Peter, now 85 and of Anchorage, remembers panning for gold with his father in an old tailing pile. They took out a few dollars in gold but the U.S. Marshal said they were trespassing and warned them to stop. Two Russian miners later acquired the land, Peter says, and recovered $40,000 from the tailings.

Bagoy's Saloon is at right in this photo of the main street of the mining camp of Discovery, in the Iditarod Mining District. John Bagoy bought his first roadhouse in Discovery in 1913. (Courtesy of the Bagoy family)

Then in 1920, Bagoy heard that gold had been found in Goodnews Bay, 260 miles southwest of Iditarod. With a friend, he assembled food and gear and set out to make his fortune. The pair ran afoul of some dangerous streams and failed to turn up any gold. Doris Bagoy Faroe, 83, of Seattle, recalls that her father later lamented that he didn't know what platinum looked like. Rich deposits of the grayish-white metal were found in the creeks of Goodnews Bay, in 1926. But neither Bagoy nor his friend recognized platinum, if indeed they saw any. Instead, says Doris, "They almost lost their lives and came home miserably defeated." But Doris' father never stayed miserable or defeated for long.

Desperate to finance their move, the Bagoys put their farm up for sale in 1921, but no one wanted to buy. Unable to sell their farm, the Bagoys instead sold raffle tickets: $5 bought a chance to win the farm! And the scheme worked. The Bagoys booked passage from Iditarod in August 1921, for two adults and five children. Their destination: the booming railroad construction town of Anchorage.

[Please see Volume 21, Number 1, The Alaska Peninsula, for a continuation of the Bagoy's saga as the family moves to Anchorage.]

WINDY CRAGGY UPDATE

Editor's note: *In* Unalaska/ Dutch Harbor, *Vol. 18, No. 4, we informed readers about potential development of a major mine in the Canadian wilderness northwest of Haines. Here's the latest on the Windy Craggy proposal.*

The British Columbia government has squelched plans by Geddes Resources Ltd. to open the huge Windy Craggy copper mine in the Alsek Range of Canada.

Instead, the government has turned 2.3 million acres, including the proposed mine site, into a provincial park off-limits to development. British Columbia also has suggested that its new park be part of a larger United Nations World Heritage Site, encompassing protected wilderness across the border in Alaska.

The park declaration drew praise from the mine's opponents, including Alaska fishermen who feared acid runoff from the mine would pollute Southeast waters and spoil upstream salmon spawning habitat. At the same time, Alaska Gov. Wally Hickel and other state officials lamented the mine's death and fretted that extending wilderness protection will further restrict resource development in Southeast.

Geddes, which had been working on the project since the mid-1980s, said it will seek financial redress from British Columbia for its investment so far, estimated at nearly $50 million.

Geddes wanted to open a combination strip and underground mine on top of 6,000-foot Windy Craggy peak. It would have been one of the largest open pit copper mines in the world.

Windy Craggy mountain, in the remote reaches of the Alsek Range of British Columbia, is about 15 miles from the Alaska border above the Tatshenshini River. The Tatshenshini is considered one of North America's wildest rivers and in 1992, was deemed worthy of preservation by the United Nations. The Tatshenshini empties into the salmon-rich Alsek River, which flows into the Pacific Ocean through the upper part of Glacier Bay National Park and Preserve.

The ambitious Windy Craggy project targeted Asian markets for the ore. Geddes proposed trucking or piping ore concentrate from the mine to Haines, Alaska, for export. Fishermen in Haines worried about possible pollution of Lutak Inlet.

Diverse groups and government agencies on both sides of the border decried Geddes' plans. Concerns included water pollution from acid drainage; location of a tailing pond in an earthquake-prone area; and industrialization of wilderness rich in wildlife, including Canada's largest concentration of grizzly bears.

Geddes maintained the mine could be developed in an environmentally sound manner.

The new park encompasses the Tatshenshini River watershed, an area twice the size of the Grand Canyon, and shares a common border with Alaska for about 100 miles, adjacent to Glacier Bay National Park. Mining, logging and road building are prohibited in the new park. Thomas Cassidy Jr., Alaska program director for American Rivers, the country's leading river-protection organization that led opposition to the mine, called British Columbia's park designation "a spectacular victory."

The Clinton administration is expected to favor inclusion of the new park in a 22-million-acre United Nations World Heritage Site, an international park joining the Tatshenshini watershed, Glacier Bay National Park and Tongass National Forest. Such U.N. designation has already been approved for Glacier Bay National Park, Wrangell-St. Elias National Park and the adjacent Kluane National Park in Canada.

United States Vice President Al Gore opposed the mine development. As a U.S. Senator, Gore had called the mine an "environmental nightmare waiting to happen."

KEEPING POLAR BEARS ALIVE

By Downs Matthews

The world's polar bears, says Dr. Dan Guravich, deserve better of mankind. Guravich has founded Polar Bears Alive to improve public attitudes toward and knowledge of the great white bears. The organization was registered in September 1992 as a non-profit public benefit corporation and is seeking support from concerned individuals and organizations.

A Canadian and biologist, Dr. Guravich spent much of his career as a professional photographer observing and photographing arctic wildlife. The experience imbued him with a strong sense of respect for polar bears. The welfare of polar bears, Guravich thinks, equates directly with the health of the global environment as observed in the far North.

Guravich created Polar Bears Alive to serve as a clearinghouse for information on the bears and as an advocate for greater understanding and better treatment for the animals.

"In today's world," Guravich says, "polar bears are not an endangered species, and we want to keep it that way."

As an organization, Polar Bears Alive will not enlist members. Its officers will serve without pay. Donations will be used to underwrite scientific research, maintain an archive of historical and current information, and support more humane treatment of polar bears wherever possible.

Interested persons may contact Polar Bears Alive, 1000 Franklin Ave., Garden City, N.Y. 11530.

BART HELPS PURCHASE VITAL GROUND

Bart, the trained brown bear, is helping buy land for grizzlies and other wild animals in the United States. Part of his earnings from his movie appearances goes to the non-profit organization Vital Ground, started two years ago by Bart's owner-trainer Doug Seus and others interested in preserving wildlife habitat. So far, Vital Ground has purchased 8,000 acres and has returned grizzlies to areas where they have long been gone.

For more information, contact Doug Seus, c/o Vital Ground, 2501 Banyon, Los Angeles, Calif., 90049.

This Ursus arctos horribilis *seems much too close for comfort, but it's only Bart, a trained brown bear on the movie set of "White Fang" during filming in Haines in 1990. Bart stands about 9 and 1/2 feet and weighs between 1,260 and 1,460 pounds, depending on the time of the year. "Bart's a pretty good comrade," says owner-trainer Doug Seus, who got the bear as a cub 16 years ago. Although Bart lives in Utah, he has Alaska lineage; his great grandfather lived on Kodiak Island and his great grandmother on Chichagof Island in Southeast. Bart knows 50 different behaviors by command. The one for this stance is simply "up." (John Hyde)*

ALASKA GEOGRAPHIC.
Newsletter

Penny Rennick,
EDITOR

Kathy Doogan,
PRODUCTION DIRECTOR

L.J. Campbell,
STAFF WRITER

Patty Bliss,
CUSTOMER SERVICE REPRESENTATIVE

Vickie Staples,
BOOKKEEPER/DATABASE MANAGER

© 1993 by The Alaska Geographic Society

McNeil River Fund, Alaska Watchable Wildlife Conservation Trust

Four new products about McNeil River brown bears are now available. Partial proceeds from the sale of these items will benefit the McNeil River Fund of the Alaska Watchable Wildlife Conservation Trust. The trust was created by the Alaska Conservation Foundation, in cooperation with the Alaska Department of Fish and Game, for wildlife enthusiasts to support enhanced viewing opportunities, research and wildlife education in Alaska.

River of Bears is biologist and writer Tom Walker's new book on McNeil, enlivened with 130 color photos by Larry Aumiller, manager of the McNeil sanctuary. Price: $35; $39.95 including postage. To order call (800) 888-9653 or write: Voyager Press, P.O. Box 338-AGS, Stillwater, Minn. 55082.

1994 River of Bears Calendar showcases spectacular color photos by Larry Aumiller. Price: $9.95. To order contact Voyager Press.

A Gathering of Bears is a 30-minute video produced by the BBC on McNeil sanctuary's brown bears. Price: $22.95. To order write Alaska Video Postcards, P.O. Box 112808-AGS, Anchorage, Alaska 99511-2808. Be sure to identify the Wildlife Trust in your order.

A panorama poster of more than 40 bears at McNeil River falls by well-known Alaska photographer Myron Wright has been scheduled for production. Contact the Alaska Department of Fish and Game, (907) 267-2179, or the Alaska Conservation Foundation, (907) 276-1917, for details.

VISITORS TO THE KNIK RIVER AREA in the Chugach Mountains east of Anchorage in 1992 and 1993 might have been surprised to see wolverines bounding across the valley. During the past two years, Kroschel Films shot 95 percent of a full-length feature, "One Paw," between Mile 7 and Mile 9 of Knik River Road; the remainder of the film was photographed in northern Minnesota. Producer and director Steve Kroschel, who filmed for the television program "Wild America" for 12 years, is working with four wolverines during this film. Kroschel says he has had a film on wolverines "in his mind since he was a kid." He says Walt Disney Studios has produced the only other films including wolverines and this footage showed "only snippets."

One Paw and fellow wolverine Skippy performed in most of the wolverine scenes for the movie. One Paw, the star, is named for a white right paw, a rare color marking for a wolverine according to Kroschel, who obtained his wolverines from Dr. Al Oeming, manager of Polar Park near Edmonton, Alberta. Polar Park has had wild-caught wolverines for years, but not until spring 1991 did the animals successfully bear young, in an event thought to be a first for captive wolverines in Canada. For the film, Kroschel used One Paw, Skippy and two cubs.

The film's human actors are all from Alaska, with the exception of the lead actress, who is from Minnesota, and Jim Fowler, of the television show "Wild Kingdom," who had a cameo appearance.

Kroschel has 10 wolverines on his farm in Minnesota where he says they do back flips, swim, climb, run, and have never bitten him or gotten

"ONE PAW" SHOOTS IN ALASKA

out of control. During the filming in the Knik Valley, One Paw, Skippy and the cubs ran up the hills, made snowballs, and generally had a good time. Kroschel has raised the wolverines from the time they were four weeks old, and speculates that their horrifying vocalizations may be what has given the wolverines such a reputation for ferociousness.

LEFT: Steve Kroschel and star wolverine, One Paw, await developments for the shooting of the next scene of Kroschel Productions' feature film, "One Paw." Steve says he spotted the potential of the Chugach Mountains near Palmer as a movie-making site while he was criss-crossing the state as a photographer for television wildlife shows. (Randy Brandon)

BELOW: Steve Kroschel plays with One Paw, one of 10 wolverines he has raised from cubs. He says the wolverines, members of the weasel family, are extremely powerful, but that he has never been bitten and that his animals have never gotten out of control. (Randy Brandon)

INDEX

[N denotes information found in the Newsletter section, pages 94-109]

A

A Gathering of Bears N108
Adverse conditioning 32
Alaska Department of Natural Resources N99
Alaska Maritime National Wildlife Refuge N95
Alaska National Interest Lands Conservation Act 87
Alaska Reindeer Act N97, N98
Alaska Watchable Wildlife Conservation Trust N108
Alaska Wildlife Serum Bank 90
Amstrup, Steven 2, 40-44, 48, 49, 54, 55
Anan Bear Observatory 57
Anan Creek 7, 10, 57, 58
  bear-viewing area 12
Arctic Institute of North America N100
Arctic National Wildlife Refuge 44, 53, 87, 92, 93
Attack avoidance 33, 71-77
Aumiller, Larry 2, 18, 27-29, 31, 32, 68, 69, N108

B

Bagoy, John N104-106
Bagoy, Marie Antoinette Vlahucic N104-106
Baker, Bruce H. 2, 5
Barnes, Vic 2, 20, 22, 29, 35, 63, 89, 92
Barrow N103
Bart N108
Bear attacks 71, 72
Bear Attacks: Their Causes and Avoidance 78
Bear habitat management 14
  "threshold" concept 14
Bear research 81-85, 87-93
Bear stereotypes 71
Bear trees 9
Bears
  black 5-15
    behavior 9

description 5
food 8
life expectancy 5
populations 13-15
range 6 (map), 7
reproduction and denning 9, 10, 12, 13
brown/grizzly 17-37
  behavior 31, 32
  cub mortality 28, 29
  description 20
  differences between brown and grizzly 17-22
  food 33-36, 66, 83
  homing instincts 22
  populations 17, 18
  range 17, 18 (map)
  reproduction and denning 23-27, 31
  weaning 29
  "cinnamon" 6, 8
  "glacier" 5
  litter size 2, 62
  polar 2, 39-55
    behavior 40, 54
    description 39, 40, 47, 50
    evolution 50
    food 40, 44, 46-49
    population 39, 43
    range 39, 43 (map)
    reproduction and denning 44-46, 53
    signs of stress 9, 32, 75, 76
    sun 20
Beier, LaVern 81-85
Bennett, Joel 47
Bevins, John 50
Blanket toss N102, N103
Brame, Judy 67
Bronson, Clark 58
Brooks Falls 17, 22, 26
Brooks Lodge 64, 66, 73
Brooks River 25, 27, 64-66, 77
Brooks, Dr. Jim 52
Brower, Eugene N101
Brower, Harry Sr. N101
Bruce, David 45
Bureau of Indian Affairs (BIA) N95, N98

C

Campbell, L.J. 2
Cape Churchill 47
"Carnivorean lethargy" 45
Carter, President Jimmy 60
Chace, Dick 69
Chilkoot Trail N104
Churchill, Manitoba 49
Clear-cutting 14
  "locus method" 14
Clebsch, Ed N102
Cornelius, Karen 75
Costello, Pat 2, 81
Cub swapping 27, 28
Cushing, Bruce 71

D

Davids, Richard C. 52
Davis, Larry N96
Dean, Fred 25, 26
Delayed implantation 31
Denali National Park 19, 23, 24, 29, 72
Denali State Park 12
Discovery N105
Drew, Slim N102

E

Eider ducks N100-103
Emmanuel, Richard P. N104

F

Fairbanks N105
Faro, Jim 67, 68
Flat N105, N106

G

Garbage bears 9, 13, 15, 73
Garner, Gerald 2, 42-44, 92
Gates of the Arctic National Park 37
Geddes Resources Ltd. N107
Glacier Bay National Park 14
Goodnews Bay N106
Gore, Vice President Al N107
Gosuk, Jacob N95
Greens Creek mine 81
Guravich, Dr. Dan N107

H

Hagemeister Island N94, N95, N97, N99

Hechtel, John 2, 87
Herrero, Stephen 78
Hessing, Pauline 29
Hickel, Gov. Wally N107
Hunting 14, 52-54, 63
  subsistence 54
Hurd, Paul N102

I

Iditarod N105, N106
International Agreement on the Conservation of Polar Bears 53
International Union for the Conservation of Nature 54

J

Jackson, Sheldon N96, N97
Jenness, Robert 46
Johnstone, Bruce 83, 85
Jonkel, Charles 19

K

Katmai National Park 17, 22, 25, 27, 64, 65, 78
Katmailand, Inc. 64, 65
Kaye, Roger 2, 87
Klondike gold rush N104
Kodiak archipelago 20, 22
Kodiak Island 24, 25, 27-29, 34, 35, 37, 43, 62, 89, 90
Kodiak National Wildlife Refuge 2, 62, 63, 92
Koranda, John N101, N102
Kroschel Films N109
Kroschel, Steve N109

L

Lane, Karl 85
LaPlant, Daniel N95
Lemmings N101, N102
Lentfer, Jack 2, 41-44, 54
Lomen and Co. N97
Lomen, Alfred N97
Lomen, Carl N97
Lomen, Ralph N97

M

Maher, Bill N101
Marine Mammal Commission 54

Marine Mammal Protection Act 42, 53, 54
Matthews, Downs N107
McCabe, Tom 93
McCutcheon, Steve 69
McDonald, Mike 71, 72, 76, 77
McNeil River 67-69
McNeil River State Game Sanctuary 2, 18, 31, 32, 61, 67
Menkens, George 50
Mikfik Creek 2, 68, 69, 75
Miller, Sterling 17, 20, 34, 36, 37
Moose 34
Muir, John 33

N

National Geographic 67, 69
Naval Arctic Research Lab N101, N102
Nome gold rush N104

O

O'Malley River 62, 63
Oeming, Dr. Al N109
Office of Naval Research N100
Old Groaner 83-85
Olson, Don N95, N99
"One Paw" N109

P

Pack Creek 59-61
Person, Dick N100, N102, N103
Petersen, Ray 64
Point Barrow N100, N103
Polar Bears Alive N107
Price, Stan 60, 61

R

Rak, Dave 57
Ray, Dorothy Jean N96, N97
Red pepper spray 78
Reindeer N94-99
Reindeer antlers N98, N99
Reindeer biology N96
Reindeer farms N98
Reindeer Herders Association N96, N98

Reindeer herders, Lapp N106
Reindeer Loan Program N95
Renecker, Lyle N99
Reynolds, Harry 20, 31, 35, 36
Rhode, Cecil 67, 69
River of Bears N108

S

"Safety in Bear Country" booklet 76
Schaefer, Paul 2, 60, 61
Schoen, Dr. John 2, 14, 37, 81
Servelo, Tom 93
Shanks, Dr. N102
Sheep, Dall 33
Sherwonit, Bill 2, 17, 57, 71, N94
Shideler, Dick 87
Soil Conservation Service N95, N98
Squirrels, arctic ground 32
St. Matthew Island reindeer herd N95
Stan Price Wildlife Sanctuary 60, 61
Stefansson, Vilhjalmur 40
Stirling, Ian 39, 47, 50
Stoneman, Jeff 58
Sues, Doug N108
Swanson, Dave N95, N98

T

Tatshenshini River N107
Tattooing 90, 91
Taylor, Paul 62, 63
The Eskimos of Bering Strait, 1650-1898 N96
Thompson, Bill N102
Thompson, Dan N101
Titus, Kim 82
Togiak N94, N95
Togiak Traditional Council N99
Tomich, Quentin N102
Tomlin, Don N98, N99
Treadwell Mine N104

U

U.S. Fish & Wildlife Service N94, N95, N99

BIBLIOGRAPHY

University of Alaska
  Fairbanks' Reindeer
  Research Program N99
University of Alaska N95
Ursidae 5
Ursus arctos
  horribilis 20, 62
  middendorffi 20, 62
  maritimus 39

V

Vital Ground N108

W

Wales N95
"Walking hibernation" 45
Whale celebration
  (*nalukataq*) N102
"White Fang" N108
Whitman, Walt N104
Williams, Tom N98
Windy Craggy mine N107
Witte, Doug N99
Wolverines N109
Wolves 36
Wrangel Island 46, 48

Y

Young, Don 87-93

PHOTOGRAPHERS

Amstrup, S.C.: 1, 39, 41,
  44, 48, 50, 53
Anderson, Cary: 8
Bagoy family: 104, 105, 106
Baker, Bruce H.: 60
Brandon, Randy: 49, 73,
  103, 109 (2)
Brandt, Craig: 31, 32
Brosamle, Sharon: 13
Burris, Fred: 24 (2)
Cornelius, Don: 15, 75
Costello, Pat: 10, 57, 78, 82,
  85
Crandall, Alissa: cover, 33,
  36, 67
Daniels, Danny: 17

DeYoung, Michael: 58 (2),
  66
Frost, Kathy/ADF&G: 45, 46
Garner, Geoff and Heidi/
  Blue Mist Photography: 27
Hyde, John/ADF&G: 59
Hyde, John: 5, 7, 12, 14, 61,
  83, 108
Kay, Charles: 76
Kaye, Roger/USFWS: 88 (2)
Lavrakas, Jim/*Anchorage
  Daily News*: 47
Lotscher, Chlaus: 37, 40
Lowry, Lloyd/ADF&G: 54
Martin, Larry/USFWS: 92
Mason, Charles: 96, 98, 99
McCutcheon, Steve: 20, 52
McWhorter, Marta: 55
Menke, David: 28, 62
Menke, Valeria: 27
Miller, Ron: 68
Nielsen, Erwin C. "Bud": 63
Peck, Lance R./Picture
  Library Associates: 6, 23
Person, Dick: 100, 101,
  102 (3)
Porter, Chip: 10
Rennick, Penny: 19, 95, 96,
  101
Riedinger, Cliff: 20, 29, 34,
  65, 78
Schliebe, Scott L./USFWS:
  42, 46, 48, 50
Schoen, John: 81, 82, 84 (2),
  85
Schooler, Lynn: 8
Sherwonit, Bill: 31
Simmen, James M.: 73
Soucek, Tom: 6, 12, 18, 26,
  75, 94, 97
Souders, Paul A. 19, 66
Speaks, Michael R.: 64, 73,
  77
Stirrup, Marion: 89, 90, 92
Syverson, Greg: 25, 71, 78
Trask, David E.: 22
Walker, Harry M.: 3, 63, 75,
  76
Warden, John W.: 32, 54,
  67, 68, 69, 72, 87, 91, 103
Wayne, Mark: 9
Young, Don/USFWS: 93

Amstrup, Steven C. "Polar Bear," *Audubon Wildlife Report 1986*, pp. 790-804. New York: The National Audubon Society, 1986.

___, Ian Stirling, Jack W. Lentfer. "Past and Present Status of Polar Bears in Alaska." From *Wildlife Society Bulletin*, Vol. 14, No. 3, Fall 1986.

___ and Oystein Wiig, eds. *Polar Bears, Proceedings of the Tenth Working Meeting of the IUCN/SSC Polar Bear Specialist Group*. International Union for Conservation of Nature and Natural Resources, 1991.

___,"Polar Bear Maternity Denning in the Beaufort Sea," *Journal of Wildlife Management*, January 1994, 58(1), in press.

___. "Human Disturbances of Denning Polar Bears In Alaska," *Arctic*, September 1993, 46 (3), in press.

___, "Masters of the Northern Ice," *ALASKA* magazine. Anchorage: Alaska Northwest Publishing, Nov. 1984.

___, Craig Gardner, Kevin C. Myers, Frederick W. Oehme. "Ethylene Glycol (Antifreeze) Poisoning in a Free-Ranging Polar Bear," from *Veterinary and Human Toxicology*, Vol. 31, No. 4, August 1989, pp. 317-319.

Aumiller, Larry and Tom Walker. *River of Bears*. Stillwater, Minn.: Voyageur Press, 1993.

Bledsoe, Thomas. *Brown Bear Summer*. New York: E.P. Dutton, 1987.

Bruce, David, Steven Amstrup, et al. "Is the Polar Bear (Ursus maritimus) a Hibernator?: Continued Studies on Opioids and Hibernation," *Pharmacology Biochemistry &*

Behavior, Vol. 35, pp. 705-711. Pergamon Press, 1990.

Chadwick, Douglas. "Grizz: Of Men and the Great Bear," in *National Geographic*, February 1986.

Craighead, Frank. *Track of the Grizzly*. San Francisco: Sierra Club Books, 1979.

Davids, Richard C. *Lords of the Arctic*. New York: Macmillan Publishing Co. Inc., 1982.

Dewey, David. *Bears*. New York: W.H. Smith Publishers, 1991.

Domico, Terry and Mark Newman. *Bears of the World*. New York: Facts on File, 1988.

Dufresne, Frank. *No Room for Bears*. Anchorage/Seattle: Alaska Northwest Books, 1991. (Originally published in 1965 by Holt, Rinehart and Winston in New York.)

Garner, Gerald, Steven T. Knick and David C. Douglas. "Seasonal Movements of Adult Female Polar Bears in the Bering and Chukchi Seas." International Conference of Bear Research and Management, 8:219-226, 1990.

Herrero, Stephen. *Bear Attacks: Their Causes and Avoidance*. New York: Nick Lyons Books, 1985.

Lentfer, Jack W., ed. *Selected Marine Mammals of Alaska, Species Accounts with Research and Management Recommendations*, "Polar Bears," pp. 41-56. Washington, D.C.: Marine Mammal Commission, 1988.

___. "Polar Bear," *Carnivora*, pp. 557-566. John Hopkins University Press, 1982.

___. "Testimony for the House Subcommittee on Fisheries and Wildlife Conservation and the Environment," on the subject of opening the Arctic National Wildlife Ref-

uge to oil and gas exploration and development. June 11, 1991.

___, convenor. Proceedings from Workshop on Measures to Assess and Mitigate the Adverse Effects of Arctic Oil and Gas Activities on Polar Bears, Anchorage, Jan. 24-25, 1989. Washington, D.C.: Marine Mammal Commission, December 1990.

___ and William A. Galster. "Mercury in Polar Bears from Alaska, *Journal of Wildlife Diseases*, 23(2), pp. 338-341. Wildlife Disease Association, 1987.

McNamee, Thomas. *The Grizzly Bear*. New York: Alfred A. Knopf, 1984.

Murie, Adolph. *The Grizzlies of Mount McKinley*. Seattle: University of Washington Press, 1985. (Originally published in 1981 by the

National Park Service.)
Proceedings of the First International Scientific Meeting on the Polar Bear. Fairbanks: U.S. Dept. of Interior Bureau of Sport Fisheries and Wildlife and the University of Alaska, 1965.

Rennicke, Jeff. *Bears of Alaska in Life and Legend*. Boulder, Colo.: Roberts Rinehart, 1987.

Rockwell, David. *Giving Voice to Bear*. Niwot, Colo.: Roberts Rinehart Publishers, 1991.

Sanders, Barry and Paul Shepherd. *The Sacred Paw: The Bear in Nature, Myth and Literature*. New York: Viking Penguin Inc., 1985.

Savage, Candace. *Grizzly Bears*. San Francisco: Sierra Club Books, 1990.

Stirling, Ian. *Polar Bears*. Ann Arbor: University of Michigan Press, 1988.

STATEMENT OF OWNERSHIP, MANAGEMENT & CIRCULATION

ALASKA GEOGRAPHIC® is a quarterly publication, home office at P.O. Box 93370, Anchorage, AK 99509. Editor is Penny Rennick. Publisher and owner is The Alaska Geographic Society, a non-profit Alaska organization, P.O. Box 93370, Anchorage, AK 99509. *ALASKA GEOGRAPHIC®* has a membership of 6,204.

Total number of copies	13,520
Paid and/or requested circulation:	
Sales through dealers, etc.	47
Mail subscriptions	6,204
Total paid and/or requested	
circulation	6,251
Free distribution	112
Copies not distributed (office	
use, returns, etc.)	7,157
TOTAL	13,520

I certify that the statement above is correct and complete.

—Vickie Staples
Bookkeeper/Database Manager

ALASKA GEOGRAPHIC® back issues

The North Slope, Vol. 1, No. 1. Charter issue. Out of print.

One Man's Wilderness, Vol. 1, No. 2. Out of print.

Admiralty...Island in Contention, Vol. 1, No. 3. $7.50.

Fisheries of the North Pacific, Vol. 1, No. 4. Out of print.

Alaska-Yukon Wild Flowers Guide, Vol. 2, No. 1. Out of print.

Richard Harrington's Yukon, Vol. 2, No. 2. Out of print.

Prince William Sound, Vol. 2, No. 3. Out of print.

Yakutat: The Turbulent Crescent, Vol. 2, No. 4. Out of print.

Glacier Bay: Old Ice, New Land, Vol. 3, No. 1. Out of print.

The Land: Eye of the Storm, Vol. 3, No. 2. Out of print.

Richard Harrington's Antarctic, Vol. 3, No. 3. $12.95.

The Silver Years, Vol. 3, No. 4. $17.95.

Alaska's Volcanoes: Northern Link In the Ring of Fire, Vol. 4, No. 1. Out of print.

The Brooks Range, Vol. 4, No. 2. Out of print.

Kodiak: Island of Change, Vol. 4, No. 3. Out of print.

Wilderness Proposals, Vol. 4, No. 4. Out of print.

Cook Inlet Country, Vol. 5, No. 1. Out of print.

Southeast: Alaska's Panhandle, Vol. 5, No. 2. Out of print.

Bristol Bay Basin, Vol. 5, No. 3. Out of print.

Alaska Whales and Whaling, Vol. 5, No. 4. $19.95.

Yukon-Kuskokwim Delta, Vol. 6, No. 1. Out of print.

Aurora Borealis, Vol. 6, No. 2. Out of stock.

Alaska's Native People, Vol. 6, No. 3. $24.95.

The Stikine River, Vol. 6, No. 4. $12.95.

Alaska's Great Interior, Vol. 7, No. 1. $17.95.

Photographic Geography of Alaska, Vol. 7, No. 2. Out of print.

The Aleutians, Vol. 7, No. 3. Out of print.

Klondike Lost, Vol. 7, No. 4. Out of print.

Wrangell-Saint Elias, Vol. 8, No. 1. $19.95.

Alaska Mammals, Vol. 8, No. 2. Out of stock.

The Kotzebue Basin, Vol. 8, No. 3. $15.95.

Alaska National Interest Lands, Vol. 8, No. 4. $17.95.

Alaska's Glaciers, Vol. 9, No. 1. Revised 1993. $19.95.

Sitka and Its Ocean/Island World, Vol. 9, No. 2. Out of stock.

Islands of the Seals: The Pribilofs, Vol. 9, No. 3. $12.95.

Alaska's Oil/Gas & Minerals Industry, Vol. 9, No. 4. $15.95.

Adventure Roads North, Vol. 10, No. 1. $17.95.

Anchorage and the Cook Inlet Basin, Vol. 10, No. 2. $17.95.

Alaska's Salmon Fisheries, Vol. 10, No. 3. $15.95.

Up the Koyukuk, Vol. 10, No. 4. $17.95.

Nome: City of the Golden Beaches, Vol. 11, No. 1. $14.95.

Alaska's Farms and Gardens, Vol. 11, No. 2. $15.95.

Chilkat River Valley, Vol. 11, No. 3. $15.95.

Alaska Steam, Vol. 11, No. 4. $14.95.

Northwest Territories, Vol. 12, No. 1. $17.95.

Alaska's Forest Resources, Vol. 12, No. 2. $16.95.

Alaska Native Arts and Crafts, Vol. 12, No. 3. $17.95.

Our Arctic Year, Vol. 12, No. 4. $15.95.

Where Mountains Meet the Sea: Alaska's Gulf Coast, Vol. 13, No. 1. $17.95.

Backcountry Alaska, Vol. 13, No. 2. $17.95.

British Columbia's Coast, Vol. 13, No. 3. $17.95.

Lake Clark/Lake Iliamna Country, Vol. 13, No. 4. Out of print.

Dogs of the North, Vol. 14, No. 1. $17.95.

South/Southeast Alaska, Vol. 14, No. 2. Out of print.

Alaska's Seward Peninsula, Vol. 14, No. 3. $15.95.

The Upper Yukon Basin, Vol. 14, No. 4. $17.95.

Glacier Bay: Icy Wilderness, Vol. 15, No. 1. Out of print.

Dawson City, Vol. 15, No. 2. $15.95.

Denali, Vol. 15, No. 3. $16.95.

The Kuskokwim River, Vol. 15, No. 4. $17.95.

Katmai Country, Vol. 16, No. 1. $17.95.

North Slope Now, Vol. 16, No. 2. $14.95.

The Tanana Basin, Vol. 16, No. 3. $17.95.

The Copper Trail, Vol. 16, No. 4. $17.95.

The Nushagak Basin, Vol. 17, No. 1. $17.95.

Juneau, Vol. 17, No. 2. Out of stock.

The Middle Yukon River, Vol. 17, No. 3. $17.95.

The Lower Yukon River, Vol. 17, No. 4. $17.95.

Alaska's Weather, Vol. 18, No. 1. $17.95.

Alaska's Volcanoes, Vol. 18, No. 2. $17.95.

Admiralty Island: Fortress of the Bears, Vol. 18, No. 3. $17.95.

Unalaska/Dutch Harbor, Vol. 18, No. 4. $17.95.

Skagway: A Legacy of Gold, Vol. 19, No. 1. $18.95.

ALASKA: The Great Land, Vol. 19, No. 2. $18.95.

Kodiak, Vol. 19, No. 3. $18.95.

Alaska's Railroads, Vol. 19, No. 4. $18.95.

Prince William Sound, Vol. 20, No. 1. $18.95.

Southeast Alaska, Vol. 20, No. 2. $19.95.

Arctic National Wildlife Refuge, Vol. 20, No. 3. $18.95.

ALL PRICES SUBJECT TO CHANGE

Your $39 membership in The Alaska Geographic Society includes four subsequent issues of *ALASKA GEOGRAPHIC*®, the Society's official quarterly. Please add $10 for non-U.S. memberships.

Additional membership information is available on request. Single copies of the *ALASKA GEOGRAPHIC*® back issues are also available. When ordering, please make payments in U.S. funds and add $2.00 postage/handling per copy book rate; $4.00 per copy for Priority Mail. Non-U.S. postage extra. Free catalog available. To order back issues send your check or money order and volumes desired to:

The Alaska Geographic Society

**P.O. Box 93370
Anchorage, AK 99509**

NEXT ISSUE: *The Alaska Peninsula*, Vol. 21, No. 1. There are perhaps as many coves and islets as there are people on the Alaska Peninsula, one of those regions in the state that exhibit the Great Land's raw geographical magnificence. Aniakchak, Veniaminof, Pavlov, active and dormant volcanoes; hidden bays, furious seas, immense offshore fisheries and hardy wildlife create a menagerie of topographical and biological splendor showcased in *The Alaska Peninsula*. To members 1994, with index. Price $19.95.